FOLLOWING JESUS

FOLLOWING JESUS

SEGUNDO GALILEA

Translated from the Spanish by
Sister Helen Phillips, M.M.

ORBIS BOOKS

Maryknoll, New York 10545

Second Printing, September 1981

The Catholic Foreign Mission Society of America (Maryknoll) recruits and trains people for overseas missionary service. Through Orbis Books Maryknoll aims to foster the international dialogue that is essential to mission. The books published, however, reflect the opinions of their authors and are not meant to represent the official position of the society.

Chapters I–V and VII–IX were first published as *El seguimiento de Cristo*, Cuadernos Testimonio, no. 7; Chapters VI and X were first published in *Espiritualidad de la liberación* (Santiago, Chile: Ed. ISPAJ, 1974); Chapter XI first appeared in *Cuestiones de espiritualidad* (Bogotá: Ed. Indoamerican Press, 1975).

Library of Congress Cataloging in Publication Data

Galilea, Segundo.
    Following Jesus.

    1. Christian life—Catholic authors—Addresses, essays, lectures. I. Title.
BX2350.2.G317513   248.4'82   80-24802
ISBN 0-88344-136-5 (pbk.)

Contents

Foreword

These pages do not claim to be a synthesis of Christology. Neither are they a systematic presentation of spirituality, nor of the Christian mysticism that ought to accompany evangelization. However, they are a little of each of these: they are spiritual conferences that have been given here and there, in different places and before a variety of audiences.

These conferences have been grouped together under a central theme: the following of Christ. It seems to us that this takes us to the root of Christianity and ought to be the basis of movements of spiritual renewal. To find Jesus Christ in the depths of the disconcerting reality that surrounds us, to follow him in the way of the Gospel until we come face to face with the Father, beyond all realities, this is the challenge to the faith of our generation.

These pages are dedicated to the Virgin Mary, mother of the church and our privileged model of the following of Jesus.

I
Conversion and Following

---

*"Simon Peter, do you love me?" . . . "Yes, Lord."
. . . "Follow me." . . . When you were young you
walked where you liked: but when you grow old . . .
somebody else will take you where you would rather
not go."* [1]

Often we cannot see the forest for the trees. The same
happens at times with spirituality. For many Catholics,
this word conjures up a multitude of demands, of beginnings, of theological ideas, that end up by covering up the
simple and essential essence of it all. Others seem to
confuse this or that important "tree" with the "forest."
They identify spirituality (and to speak of spirituality is to
speak of Christian life) with prayer, or with the cross, or
with a complete dedication to others.

The Gospel reveals to us the basis of all spirituality and
gives back to us the demanding simplicity of Christian
identity. It teaches us that to be a disciple of Jesus is to
follow him, and that this is what Christian life is. Jesus
basically demanded that we follow him, and all our Christianity is built on our response to this call. [2] Since then the
essence of Christian spirituality has been the following of
Christ under the guidance of the church.

To be a Christian is to follow Christ out of love. It is

1

Jesus who asks us if we love him; it is we who answer that we do. It is he who invites us to follow him: "Simon Peter, do you love me? . . . Yes, Lord. . . . Then follow me."[3] And that's all. Just as simple as that. Although we are ignorant, full of failings, Jesus will lead us to sanctity, provided that we begin by loving him and that we have the courage to follow him.

Christianity does not consist only in a knowledge of Jesus and of his teachings transmitted by the church. It consists in following him. Only in this way can we prove our faithfulness. Following him is the root of all Christian demands and is the only criterion by which we can evaluate our spirituality. Therefore, there does not exist a "spirituality of the cross," but one of following him—a following that at times will demand the cross of us. There does not exist a "spirituality of prayer," but one of following him. This following will lead us to join in the prayer of the one whom we follow. There does not exist a "spirituality of poverty," but one of following. It will strip us bare if we are faithful in following a God of poverty. There does not exist a "spirituality of commitment," for all commitment or dedication to others is the fruit of our faithfulness to the way that Jesus followed.

To follow Christ implies the decision of submitting all other following on earth to the following of God made flesh. Therefore to speak of the following of Christ is to speak of conversion, of "selling all," to use the evangelical expression, in order to acquire that pearl and that hidden treasure which is the following of Jesus.[4] Only God can demand such a following and it is in following Jesus that we follow God, the only Absolute.

All Christians know what conversion is: to conform ourselves to the values that Christ taught, which bring us out of our egoism, injustice, and pride. We also know that conversion is the foundation of all Christian fidelity in our personal lives, in the apostolate, or in social, professional, and political involvement. Conversion pulls us out of our hiding places and takes us "where we would rather not go" in following Christ.

We are not always conscious of the autonomous character of conversion. This evangelical, universal demand has nothing to do with level of education or of culture or with social position. It has nothing to do with power or with wealth or with knowledge or with any type of activity, involvement, or ideology. "Professional" converts or "classes" of converts do not exist. Nor does being a religious, bishop, or cardinal necessarily presuppose conversion, which has its own unique demands.

All Christians, whatever their status, secular or ecclesiastical, are permanently called to the dynamism of their conversion in which there are no privileges or respect for persons, and which radically depends on our response to the call of Christ. This response conditions every human and ecclesial project and is the only authentic verification of any commitment. "On the day of judgment many will say to me, 'Lord, Lord, we have prophesied in your name and in your name we have driven out demons and in your name we have worked many miracles.' And I will say to them: 'I do not know you. Depart from me all you evildoers.' "

"But he who listens to my words and acts on them is like a sensible man who built his house upon a rock. The rains came down, floods rose, gales blew and hurled themselves against the house, but the house did not fall because it was built upon rock. . . ."[5]

We are not always aware of the path of conversion, or of its unique dynamism. Christ does not call us only once during our lives. We receive many calls. Each one is more demanding than the last and is part of the great crises of our human-Christian growth. Conversion is a process that calls us to a radical evangelical life in our "world" in order to live the exodus of our faith and to follow the Lord.

The Gospel shows us this critical process in the lives of the disciples of Jesus, perhaps most notably in the spiritual development of Peter.

We can place the conversion of Peter to the ranks of the Lord at the time of the miraculous draft of fishes related in St. Luke.[6] The text is well known. Jesus had just finished preaching from the boat to a great crowd of people on the shores of the Lake of Galilee. Among his listeners were Peter and some other future apostles. Up until then they had followed Christ from afar, in the midst of their chores as fishermen, without having been called as yet to a more radical way of following him.[7]

Having finished his discourse, Jesus invites them to go fishing. They had done just that all night but without success. Peter, full of confidence in Christ's word that he had learned to accept, returns to the lake to cast out the nets. The catch is extraordinary and they return to the shore. Peter realizes that before him is one who is more than just a wise preacher. This clashes with the awareness of his own wretchedness and throws him into internal conflict; kneeling down before Jesus he asks him to go away from him because he knows he himself is a sinner. But the Lord takes advantage of Peter's crisis of conscience to call him to conversion: "Don't be afraid, from now on you will be a fisher of men."

Peter gives himself completely to Christ. The sign of his conversion and that of his companions is that "they left all and followed Jesus."[8]

At first glance it seems like a total conversion. But in the attitudes of Peter during Jesus' public life we can see that his journey toward conversion was still in its beginnings. In him there is great generosity, enthusiasm, impulsiveness, and a great feeling of love for the Lord. However, there is also an excess of confidence in himself and in his capabilities. His idea of Christ and of the kingdom to which he had given himself was still superficial. His commitment contained much of the ambiguity characteristic of many of the Israelites of his day: Jesus for him was not only a religious master but also the earthly Messiah who would liberate Palestine. Only after three years of ministry does Peter recognize in Jesus the Son of God,[9] but the nature of the kingdom still eludes him. "Fisher of men" had for him and his companions the notion of an earthly kingdom in which they would exercise influence and authority. That is why they fought over the first places[10] and even to the hour of the Resurrection they hoped for the restoration of Israel.[11]

This is why Peter has more and more difficulty in understanding the nature of discipleship. When Jesus speaks of the cross, he is shocked.[12] He is incapable of freeing those possessed by the devil as his Master has done, because he still has not understood the value of faith and of prayer.[13] During the hours of the Passion he experiences his limitations in a dramatic way, as well as the precariousness of his commitment and conversion. Full of emotional fervor, he had announced that he would never abandon the Master even if everyone else did.[14] Not many hours later he repeatedly denied and betrayed his Lord.

For Peter this was a serious crisis. It made him understand the superficiality of his conversion. His self-sufficiency and human respect crumbled.

But Jesus takes advantage of this very crisis to call him again to a more mature and decisive conversion. This scene takes place in the accounts of the resurrection given to us by St. John.[15] It is very much like his first call. The setting is the same, the Lake of Galilee, and the circumstances very similar. Peter and other apostles are fishing and they have caught nothing all night long. At daybreak, Jesus, standing on the shore, tells them to cast their nets to the right of the boat; and they do make an enormous catch of large fishes. Then they all come ashore to eat with Jesus.

When the meal is over Jesus again talks to Peter as he did some years before and calls on him to follow him, this time in the form of a triple question: "Simon, do you love me more than these? . . . Yes, Lord, you know that I love you. . . . Feed my sheep."[16]

Peter has been able to overcome his crises and to say "yes" to Jesus, but the crises have taught him much. They allow him to make a response more mature, deeper, and qualitatively different from that of three years before. Apparently he has lost enthusiasm, and the generosity and spontaneity of before. Now he does not dare to declare as he had before the Passion that he loves Christ more than the rest.

Now he is aware of his limits and of his faults and this knowledge has made him more humble. Now his commitment is no longer based upon his own capabilities but rather on the word of Jesus who has called him. He seems less enthusiastic and committed but in reality it is now that his conversion is clearer and deeper. Now he commits himself with a knowledge of the cause of a crucified Lord and a kingdom that is not of this world and which is built on faith. Peter is ripe to follow Christ with no illusions or sentimentalism, in the maturity and depth of his life of faith. Previously he had left his house, his boats, his work, but had never really given up himself. That's why Jesus completes his call with this announcement: "When you were young, you girded yourself and walked where you liked; but when you grow old, you will stretch out your hands and somebody else will gird you and will take you where you would rather not go."[17]

The discipleship of Peter, from his superficial first conversion to his later more mature one of faith through crisis, is a paradigm of the conversion process of every Christian. Like Peter we also at some moment of our life hear our first call to conversion. We decide to take our Christianity seriously and in many cases to follow Christ with a total dedication. Each of us knows when that moment was, most likely in our youth.

Like the apostles we became disciples "abandoning boats and nets" and in some cases even families. It seemed to us then the height of generosity. Everything contributed to this idea of discipleship; it was most attractive and seemed so realizable. The Lord's presence was felt and our prayer brought us the consolation that helped us to face the difficulties of living out our apostolate in which Jesus was "felt" as our support and inspiration.

This apostolic and social commitment "filled" us. Even with little experience everything at first was new, a fascinating discovery of service to others. We wanted to place no limits to our charity and sacrifice, which "fulfilled" us and which was its own recompense. Evangelical poverty had its own aura, even a certain romanticism. If we had chosen celibacy this brought with it renunciation and difficulties, but all were tolerable through the presence of Christ and of his evangelical ideal, so strongly felt in our hearts.

With time, everything gradually changed. A kind of crisis loomed up, at times sudden, usually progressive and slow. The moment when this happened, the enthusiasm of our first fervor was beclouded. It was not the same for all of us. Some months, some years, or many years later, our life of faith is invaded by a growing insensitivity. The evangelical values upon which our conversion was based begin to lose their meaning and the emotional attraction which they once had for us. We feel the presence of Christ in our lives and especially in our prayers less and less; instead we feel a dryness, a loneliness, a darkness that takes us farther and farther from the face of the Lord.

Prayer no longer provides us with the old emotional support; instead it tires us and leaves us dry. It doesn't seem to have any influence in our lives or in our activities. It now seems that whether or not we pray all will remain the same: ourselves, our commitments, other people, history. That's why one of the first temptations is to abandon our personal prayer.

Our apostolic or social commitments lose all their novelty; they become routine. The tasks and problems that we have to face seem boringly repetitious and we find ourselves speaking of the same thing over and over. Human nature looks the same to us everywhere. We begin to feel disappointments, failures; we feel that all our efforts are unimportant if not useless. Difficulties, obstacles, and persecutions begin to multiply, coming at times from where we least expect them, even from those with whom we work and from ecclesiastical authorities. We become tired; we yearn for independence, to do something more interesting, to make our own lives. There is a desire to "settle down," to do only what is indispensable, without searching, without changing, without creativity.

Poverty and sacrifice become increasingly difficult. They have lost their original attraction, and more than this, they have not been appreciated as we have thought they would have been. We have been misinterpreted, judged "excessive." Besides, as the years go by we become more demanding, more bourgeois. We look for security and a "minimum of comfort."

We now begin to resent our first impulse toward charity and the service of others. As time goes on we realize the difficulty of that demand, above all when there is no longer an emotional support and we no longer know how to love. Our own dispositional limitations which we have not been able to shake off become more and more accentuated as the years go by, with the danger that they begin to take over more and more as we grow older.

For those who have chosen celibacy, chastity also becomes complicated. At each stage of life we become more aware of new demands not foreseen in our youth. We must accept not only the renunciation of intimacy with the opposite sex but also the extension of ourselves in other human beings, the loving atmosphere of a home; we must accept a form of radical solitude.

The great temptation of this crisis is that of compromise. We look for some comfortable position somewhere between the Gospel and the "world," between holiness and indispensable fidelity, so that while we display a sincere exterior, something that appears "intact," we have closed in upon ourselves, losing all the dynamism of discipleship and love. We tend to introduce into our lives derivatives of and substitutions for the Gospel. A certain conformity is assumed, a desire for a career, to transform Christian radicalism into "careful prudence." We seek positions, exterior prestige, with no consideration as to whether this corresponds to the demands that Jesus makes upon our lives.

It is the temptation of discouragement. Perhaps for the first time we truly understand the words that Jesus spoke to his apostles: "What is impossible for human beings is possible for God."[18]

It is precisely this crisis of Christian discipleship, dramatic and subtle, that prepares us for and leads us to a more mature and decisive conversion. Like Peter after the Passion, after his crisis, disorientation, and insensitivity, Jesus calls us again.

It is important to know how to approach the normal stages proper to the dynamics of a conversion. They place us once again before the crucial alternative: either remain in a discouraged and mediocre state or choose again, more lucidly and maturely, the radicalism of the Gospel. Jesus leads us to a conversion in a profound and adult faith that goes beyond the emotional enthusiasm of a first conversion. We ought not to compare the different stages of our lives: through normal development generosity, prayer, commitment, and poverty gradually become purified. From a basis in feeling, in good will, and in personal capabilities, they mature to the point where all is based on the word of Christ and on the demands of the Gospel united within us in faith.

This brings us to another form of discipleship more deeply rooted in the cause of the Gospel and less in feelings or in an unconscious desire for self-advancement and influence. It leads us to another type of prayer, less emotional and sought after for psychological motives, more strongly based on the following of Christ that unites us to his liberating prayer. It leads us to another kind of poverty, less external and concerned with "witness value," and more of a strong solidarity with the Christ of the poor and with the oppressed.

Chastity, always difficult, continually develops into a universal friendship and fidelity to an exclusive love of the Lord. We shall be capable of beginning each day with a new apprenticeship in fraternal love, not through the feeling of affection that this might give us but rather in the service of Jesus who lives in all of us.

Our feelings and senses may reappear and help us to a greater or lesser degree in our evangelical convictions, but they will adhere more to the options of a purified charity and a radical faith that will impel us like the apostles to be "witnesses of the Gospel . . . to the ends of the earth."[19]

We have to know how to develop and grow in the stages of crisis that mark the great conversions of life. Basically they are opportunities to rediscover the great values that attracted us at the beginning, but now appear under a new light. We must ourselves continue praying, giving to others, working and hoping, in a certain darkness and dryness, inspired by our convictions of faith.

The true Christian conversion is one of faith. Only through faith are we able to take the radical step of giving ourselves unreservedly to the word of Jesus. Like Peter we can give up our work and everything else, but deep down we are self-centered. We hang on to our lives. ". . . He who clings to his life loses it, and he who scorns his life in this world will keep it for eternal life."[20]

The mature conversion does not consist so much in "feeling" our discipleship, or in multiplying acts of generosity, but rather in allowing ourselves to be led by the Lord in faith, on the cross, and in hope. "When you were young, you girded yourself and walked where you liked; but when you grow old, you will stretch out your hands and somebody else will gird you and take you where you would rather not go."[21]

II

The Face of Jesus

---

*And the word was made flesh and dwelt among us
and we have seen his glory, the glory as of the only
Son of the Father. In him was all love and fidelity.
. . . In him was the fullness of God and we receive all
from him. . . .* [1]

The originality and authenticity of Christian spirituality
consists in this: that we follow a God who took upon
himself our human condition, One who had a history like
ours, who lived our experiences, who made choices, who
devoted himself to a cause for which he suffered, who had
successes, joys, and failures, for which he gave his life.
That man, Jesus of Nazareth, like us in all except sin, in
whom lived the fullness of God, is the only model for our
discipleship.

For this reason the starting point of our Christian
spirituality is the encounter with the humanity of Jesus.
This is what gives Christian spirituality all its realism. In
making the historical Jesus the model of our discipleship,
Catholic spirituality uproots us from the illusion of
"spiritualism," of an "idealistic" Christianity, of values
that are abstract and alien to historical experiences and
demands. It frees us from the temptation of adapting Jesus
to *our* image, to *our* ideals, to *our* interests.

Our spirituality has to recover the historical Christ. This dimension has frequently been played down in our Latin American tradition. This tradition has a tendency to "dehumanize" Jesus Christ, to emphasize his divinity without giving enough emphasis to his humanity, with all the consequences. This tendency has brought with it many consequences. The Jesus of "power," extraordinary, miraculous, purely divine, hides Jesus as a historical model of discipleship.

It is only through Jesus of Nazareth that we can know God, his words, his deeds, his ideals, his demands. It is in Jesus that the true God reveals himself: all-powerful but at the same time poor and suffering for love; absolute, but also someone with his own human history, someone close to every person.

Only in the historical Jesus can we truly come to know the values of our own Christian life. There is always the danger of formulating these values from fixed ideas and definitions: "prayer is this . . .," "poverty consists in this other . . .," "fraternal love has these certain characteristics. . . ." But just as we don't know who God is unless we discover him through Jesus, we can never really know what prayer is, what poverty is, what fraternity or celibacy is except in the way Jesus came to know these values. Jesus is not only a model of living; he is the root of the values of life.

Thus any real following of Christ springs from a knowledge of his humanity, his personality traits, his way of acting, which by themselves make up the demands of our Christian life.

This knowledge does not come from biblical science or theology, but rather from an encounter in faith and in love, which are proper to the wisdom of the Spirit and of Christian contemplation. It comes from knowing the Lord whom we follow "contemplatively" with all our being, especially with all our heart—as disciples, not as students; as followers, not as investigators. Here we again see the essence of Christian spirituality: we know Jesus only to the extent that we try to follow him. The face of the Lord is revealed to us in the experience of discipleship. For this reason Catholic Christology is a contemplative Christology that puts into practice the imitation of Jesus.

Now let us not think that this contemplative and imitative knowledge of Jesus is easy. It goes beyond analysis and reason. St. Paul speaks to us of a "hidden wisdom that comes from God,"[2] and he also tells us that "he counted everything as loss"[3] to him in comparison to this knowledge of the Lord.[4] The revelation of Christ in us, the contemplative Christology of which we speak, is a gift of the Father. To receive this as wisdom and not just as knowledge demands of us a great poverty of spirit along with the gifts of the Holy Spirit, who breathes where it will.

We can prepare for this contemplative revelation of Jesus by immersing ourselves in faith in the Gospel and by disposing ourselves as disciples in order to learn what this Word teaches us about the Lord. We can have a solid Christology and exegesis but these can never take the place of the contemplation of the Gospel. The Gospel transmits to us what most deeply impressed the apostles and the first disciples; it was brought together in the tradition of the first communities to recall what was most significant for the faith and spirit of the Christians. "What we have heard with our ears and seen with our eyes, what we have looked upon and touched with our hands concerning the word of life, we proclaim also to you. . . ."[5]

For this reason the Gospel is irreplaceable. We find in it Christology as wisdom, and the image of Christ as the inspiring message of all discipleship. We find there a person whom we can imitate out of love. This contemplative love of itself leads us constantly to the imitation of Jesus, which is the best guarantee of discipleship.

This does not imply falling into a literal mimicry of the historical Jesus of the Gospel, thus forgetting that our imitation before all else refers to the Christ of faith communicated by the church. Actually this Christ of faith that the church presents to us is in continuity with the Christ of the Gospel. He in turn guarantees the objectivity of our contemplation, which rightly bases itself on the Gospel given us through the church as a stimulus for our conversion.

When we try to determine the human image of Jesus and his Christological message, we find ourselves faced with a task that doesn't really admit of any definite solution. At least, the personality given us in the Gospels is impossible to understand and to penetrate. It is so radically paradoxical and different from anything that we know that it defies any classification. Just when we think that we know him, he appears in another way, with new traits that we had not discovered and that blur our previous outline. To contemplate Christ introduces us to an inexhaustible personality.

Even so, each of us has a personal idea of the Lord more or less well founded, more or less unconscious, forming part of a Christology that influences our very being and all our actions as Christians.

Even though we don't notice it, into this image that we make of the personality of Jesus goes our own manner of being, our own psychology, and the various forms of our egoism. We are always in danger of deforming, according to our own conditioning, the real personality of the Lord. We tend to shape Jesus in our own image and likeness, according to our measure, justifying our mediocrity and infidelity to adapt the message of the person of Christ to us and not us to him. The only way to avoid this constant

temptation will be the permanent return to the contemplation of the Christ of the Gospels. Otherwise we shall
transform Christology into a projection of ourselves and
Christian praxis into an ideology in which we accept the
aspects of the Gospel that fit into an already adopted
personal position or ideology.

What is the message of the Gospel about the person of
the Lord?

In the first place it presents to us the *religious dimension
of Jesus:* a person profoundly united to the Father, in
communication with him, dependent on his will, a man
who constantly cultivated this intimacy and whose prayer
clearly demonstrates this. The prayer of Christ is impressive. In the midst of his activities he often went apart to
pray, and he passed whole nights in prayer.[6] The crucial
moments of his life, particularly those in which he was
tempted, were marked by long periods of prayer (the fast
of forty days, Gethsemane . . .). Jesus was completely
dedicated to the Father.

This dedication, always expressed in his prayer, transcends his personal or cultural situation. Jesus really
prayed, as a need of his humanity to communicate with his
Father and to express his love for him. In this he is perfectly human. This communication with the divine absolute is proper to human nature and the possibility of realiz-
ing it is not tied to a pre-technological culture or "rural"
religious practices (of the Palestine of that time). The
relationship of Jesus with his Father is natural to him and
not cultural; it transcends the contingencies of an era and
of religious practice.

This contemplative life of Jesus that was so central to
his person did not separate him or make him alien to other
people, or to human conflicts, or replace his mission. Just
as Jesus is the man of God, he is at the same time *a man
among men,* the "man for everyone." The Gospel is as

significant in this aspect as in the former. This prophet, this teacher, this wonderworker, this man of God was absolutely approachable. The crowds followed him and surrounded him, and the times when he escaped from them he gave himself completely to the apostles and disciples. He did not withdraw, he never put up any barriers, he never inhibited anyone.[7] He inspired confidence so that they could approach him whenever they wanted to, even to the point where his activity seemed made up more of interruptions and the unexpected than of his own plans. His plans were destroyed by his attitude of total commitment, even to the extent that he did not have time to eat, and he often had to flee.[8]

This is the great paradox of Jesus, and in this he remains as an inexhaustible norm of discipleship. All of us are a little unbalanced in this aspect, conditioned by our temperament and ideology. We tend to make Christianity either markedly transcendent (related to God) or incarnate (committed to our neighbor), disregarding one or other dimension. It is not sufficient to try to solve our problem by talking of the theology of the two natures in the person of Christ. We must contemplate, even to imitation, the actions of Jesus, and this imitation out of love will bring us to a stability and equilibrium that only he can teach us. He is the only master, master of the synthesis of contemplation and commitment, of the absorption in God's absolute, and of the giving of ourselves to others without reserve.[9]

Jesus is also the model of discipleship in the quality of his commitment. In him this is personalized and takes the form of the *gift of his friendship*. Jesus did not have a mass pastoral plan. He treated each and every one as unique and special[10] and gave to all his full attention and friendship, in a universal way. His friendliness protects the children[11] and frees the woman.[12] Breaking through the prejudices of his time, he gives himself to sinners, the sick, prostitutes, publicans, tax collectors, soldiers, government officials, the poor, the slaves. . . . Judas himself, who for some time hadn't believed in him, he treats as a friend until the end ("Friend, with a kiss you betray the Son of Man . . ."[13]). This expression on the lips of Jesus is not sarcasm.

The brotherly welcome that Jesus offered to everyone is a model for us. We must practice this realistically, without illusions or naiveté, just as Christ did, he "who was not deceived because he knew very well what was in the heart of every man,"[14] and yet gave himself with limitless charity. This fraternal love of Jesus brought him no great compensations. He always remained a man radically alone and misunderstood, until the resurrection. He knew how to balance once again, in an admirable synthesis, the loneliness of the prophet with the love of a brother.

Another characteristic of the human personality of Jesus is the *attractiveness of his message*. This is of great significance for today's pastoral activity and for the force of evangelization. It is not enough that the message which we preach be true; it is necessary that it attract people to conversion and lead them on to discipleship, as was the case with Jesus. After the Sermon on the Mount, as related by St. Matthew, everyone was astonished because he did not speak as the scribes and Pharisees but as "one who had authority."[15] "Never has anyone spoken as that man. . . ."

It is amazing to see the impact and the attraction of a word that has lasted for centuries, that transformed people and societies, and that today is a source of inspiration for millions of human beings. It is amazing because it was spoken by the son of a carpenter in the context of a very simple culture, foreign to the then current philosophies and dominant religions. It was spoken in a very simple way, using examples and parables from daily life, at a time when both political and religious speakers were multiplying. But there was "something special"in his message that made them say that no one had ever spoken like this man. This was all the more notable because Jesus explicitly rejected the political leadership and oratory in circumstances where that leadership was a source of prestige before the Roman situation.

This attractiveness of the Lord was due to the harmony between his person, his deeds, and his words. His sincerity and loyalty were so obvious that his word was seen as decisive, for good or for ill, as acceptance or rejection—without forgetting that the words of Jesus, as with those of everyone, were subject to a wrong interpretation and to ambiguity. His message was also manipulated, and although he announced the kingdom of God, at the end of his life the Sanhedrin and the Roman power accused him as a politician and subversive. "If this man goes on talking this way, everyone will go off with him, and the Romans will come and destroy our holy place and our nation."[16] It is well known that the announcement of the kingdom—pastoral activity—by its very nature has a dimension of social criticism so that for the pastor and the prophet it becomes a source of conflict and misunderstanding. For constituted power, which would like to reduce the message to the private realm, this is too much; it is ambiguous, illegitimately political. Jesus accepted and assumed the consequences of the social conflict of his message. In this he also teaches us a pastoral wisdom.

The personality of Jesus is characterized also by *fidelity to his mission*. This is one of the most impressive qualities of the Gospel. Jesus has a goal, an ideal, a commitment, and he follows them to the end. Nothing makes him deviate from his mission, not failures, misunderstandings, loneliness, abandonment by his friends and disciples; not the cross or—above all—the temptation that came to him during his public life to use his divine power in the fulfillment of his mission, and not the way of kenosis.[17]

Fidelity to his mission brought him to crisis upon crisis until it culminated in the dark loneliness of the crucifixion. In Capernaum, when the announcement of the Eucharist scandalizes his hearers and many abandon him, he looks for support to the Twelve. But at the same time he lets it be known that nothing would swerve him from his mission, and that he was ready to go on alone. "Do you also perhaps wish to leave me?" Peter answered: "Lord, who would we go to? You have words of eternal life. We believe and we know that you are the Holy One of God. . . ."[18] In all of this there is not a trace of bitterness, discouragement, or scepticism in Jesus. He is consumed by an ideal and pierced by his commitment to the Father and to all men and women, and this love in him is greater than the temporary support of others and the hardness of heart that he sees in those closest to him. They accepted him but never fully understood him. In Jesus we see united the universality of a mission and the loneliness of the prophet. Only the light of Christian contemplation and the gift of the Spirit given to us as wisdom through contact with the Lord allow us to penetrate this mysterious and paradoxical attitude of self-emptying faithful unto death. We know intuitively that this is essential to discipleship and that the commitment of our life constitutes the essence of the apostolate.

In his mission, *Jesus knew how to wait for God's own time* as regards people and events. This is wisdom and not pastoral knowledge. Christ was the master and the teacher who waited respectfully for people to mature, never using undue power to convert them and make them understand. His attitude toward the twelve apostles is a brilliant example of pastoral wisdom. He accepted them with their slowness, their contradictions and hardness, without giving up on their formation and preparation in view of the future. He never judged, never imposed himself; rather he extended an invitation: "If you wish . . . if you are ready. . . ." He did not take advantage of his leadership or of his power to force the normal development of their rights.

From this we see the paradox of a Gospel that appears at the same time extremely demanding and always understanding. Demand and understanding are perfectly balanced in Jesus. At times the ideal proposed seems almost inhuman; only God could propose or demand such things. "He who would be my disciple must deny himself, take up his cross every day and follow me . . . If you would follow me, sell all that you have . . . No one can be my disciple if he doesn't give up all that he possesses. . . . If your hand scandalizes you, cut it off. . . . Unless the grain of wheat dies, only it remains . . . He who loves his life will lose it and he who scorns his life in this world will keep it unto life eternal . . . Love one another . . . Be perfect like your heavenly Father . . . Which of the three was a neighbor to the injured man?. . . Go and do likewise . . ."

These and other demands present us with a radical option that is all but totally overwhelming. Nevertheless, and this is the paradox, no one who really contemplated the Christ of the Gospels ever felt crushed or discouraged by these demands. They are so filled with love, with confidence, with freedom, and with the inspiring example of him who lived them out first and who gave himself that we might also live them, that they are a constant invitation to growth and to overcoming. The Gospel, with all its strength and demands, gives us the impression of a comprehension and humanity of such quality that it frees us. Thus Christians, who flee from other types of demands because they feel oppressed by them, go to the Gospel and to Christ, where the demands are much greater. But the

Gospel demands lead us to love more and to be more free. This is the secret of why the Christian ethic is always valid. At times it seems difficult and inhuman, at times sentimental. At times it seems revolutionary, made for great things, at times, on the other hand, like a cry of support for the weak and the "little ones." At times unattainable, and at times made for everyone.

If the evangelical demands lead us to the freedom of love and to a poverty of self-forgetfulness, it is because the person who sets these forth is *himself free and poor and forgetful of self.* Free because he is poor, Jesus appears as such before the Father, before the rest of humanity, and before himself.

His total and free abandonment into the hands of the Father is demonstrated by his fidelity to his mission[19] and his detachment from every kind of necessity by the humble acceptance of his personal history, of the place and circumstances of his life, of the people who surrounded him and followed him by the acceptance of his road of kenosis, of his servant role, of abandonment by all. Friend of all, he allowed no one to monopolize him. His freedom was as great as his gift of himself. He avoids the line of facile leadership, of the marvelous, of the spectacular, in spite of his miracles, which he tried to have pass unnoticed.

The radical poverty of his kenosis has permitted Jesus to set free the poor, to understand real poverty, and to declare it blessed. He welcomes sinners and grants them his mercy in abundance. He gives privileges "to the least of our brothers."[20] These attitudes were all possible to him because he himself was a poor man who lived the beatitudes, and in contemplating the Father he learned the real wisdom of God, "a wiser madness than the wisdom of men."[21] He learned the ways of God, the preferences of the Father, and also his dislikes (e.g. Phariseeism and hypocrisy). "He who sees me sees the Father."[22] In Jesus we can know the plan of God in its most human and incarnate expression, and we begin to know the criteria of God: his mercy, his search for the lost sheep, his predilection for the "little ones," his tendency to personalize, his missionary zeal to find what is lost, his demands. . . .

We could go on contemplating the characteristics of him who with good reason we call Lord and Master. They not only make up his personality but also his way of acting, his pastoral action. This "contemplative Christology" not only gives form to our Christian being; it is also the norm of our discipleship.

III

Following Jesus
in My Brothers and Sisters

. . . The Doctor of the Law answered: "You must love the Lord your God with all your heart, with all your soul, with all your strength and with all your might; and your neighbor as yourself." Jesus said to him: "You have answered well; do this and you will live." But the man wanting to justify himself said to Jesus: "Who is my neighbor?" [1]

The preaching of Jesus, whose central theme is the kingdom of God, has for its object to make all people brothers and sisters. It revealed to us that God is our Father, making of this common fatherhood the root of our fraternity. This is a real possibility since Christ appears in history as our universal brother.

By insisting absolutely on fraternal love and on the fact that we are brothers and sisters,[2] and by stressing the second commandment of the Law ("Love your neighbor as yourself"; "Love one another as I have loved you "[3]) he has made the love of neighbor the mark of Christian identity, the decisive proof of our discipleship.

His hearers no doubt asked whom the master considered a neighbor, how far he extended this idea, and how one had to live this out concretely in daily life. Undoubtedly Jesus went much further than the Old Testament concept in which the neighbor (or brother) was a friend, one who shared the religion and the nationality of the Jews. The urgency to be precise about "who is my neighbor," whom we must love in deed and not just in words, I believe is just as important today for Christians and for those who without being Christians accept this basic demand of Jesus.

Who are our neighbors in the concrete circumstances of our personal history? Are they our friends? Christians? Our fellow citizens? Or are they also the inhabitants of other countries (whom we never see), that is to say, everybody?

This question, which especially disturbed the most critical of Jesus' hearers, comes from the lips of a doctor of the Law as a question and a test of the idea of neighbor that Jesus was preaching. "In order to put him to the test,"[4] the lawyer asked him about the second commandment of the Law, which was like the first, "Love your neighbor as yourself." But that was not the decisive question. What interested the doctor of the Law was the idea that Jesus had about the "neighbor," an idea that until now was apparently never clearly explained: "Wanting to give the reason for his question, he said to Jesus: "Who is my neighbor?"[5]

Jesus does not respond with a definition, but with a parable, with a story with which we can all identify. The essence of every Gospel story is that we can identify with the people in the story. That's why it has universal and timeless value. In this case the story is the parable of the good Samaritan, and the consequences put forth here regarding the neighbor are valid for all of us. The "go and do likewise"[6] is a counsel given not only to the doctor of the Law but also to us.

Meditation on this parable will lead us to a discovery of who my neighbor is according to Jesus' criteria.[7]

THE NEIGHBOR AS THE POOR PERSON

My neighbor is anyone who has a right to expect something from me, the one who God puts in the way of my own personal history. In some way every human being is potentially my neighbor (even those who live on another continent and whom I have never met), but really and historically my neighbor is the one whom I meet in my life, since only in this case is there a right to an act of fraternal love. Christian brotherhood is a willingness to make anybody my neighbor if the occasion presents itself.

My neighbor is the one in need. In the parable of the good Samaritan the needy one is the Jew who has been beaten and robbed. In the parable of the Last Judgment[8] the needy one is the hungry and the thirsty, the sick, the abandoned, the imprisoned. In a very special way, the neighbor is the poor person, in whom Jesus reveals himself as the needy one. "Whatever you did to some of the least of my brothers, you did to me."[9]

There are temporarily needy and permanently needy (poor). We do not know if the wounded Jew of the parable was sociologically poor; we can even presume that he wasn't, since if he was robbed it was because he had money on him. But at the moment of his meeting with the Samaritan he was poor and needy. He had the right to be treated as a neighbor. The rich and the powerful are my neighbors when they have need of me, even if this is only on occasion. It is a Christian duty to give aid to capitalists or to political leaders persecuted because of political changes, whatever their ideologies. This is to treat them as neighbors.

But the majority are permanently poor and needy. They

are exploited, pushed aside, and made poor by society. They are discriminated against by ideological systems and by the great powers. The option for the poor which the Gospel mandates is to serve our neighbors not only as people but also as social situations. Today our neighbor is also collective. The wounded and despoiled Jew is a permanent situation. They are the workers, the *campesinos*, the Indians, the subproletariat. . . .

The Christian option is not for poverty, because poverty as such does not exist. The option is for the poor, above all for the permanently poor in my path and part of my society, the one who has the right to expect something from me. The fact of the poor as a collective neighbor gives to fraternal charity its great social and political demand. For the Gospel the socio-political commitment of the Christian is because of the poor person. Politics means the liberation of the needy.

THE REQUIREMENT OF "BECOMING A BROTHER"

When he finished telling the parable to the doctor of the Law, Jesus asked him a question that might surprise us: "Which of these three acted like a neighbor [brother] to the man who fell into the hands of the robbers?"[10] This means that all three were not brothers to the wounded one. They could have been, but in fact it was "the one who showed him compassion."[11] The priest was not a brother to the Jew nor was the Levite. The Samaritan was. For Jesus, to be brother to the others is not something automatic, like an acquired right. We are not brothers to others if we do not act as such. We must make ourselves brothers to all.

Christianity does not teach us that in fact we are already brothers. That would be to teach us something unreal. The experience of hatred, division, injustice, and violence that we see each day tells us just the opposite. We are not brothers but we can become so. That is the teaching and the capability that the Gospel gives us. Jesus demands this of us and he gives us the strength to "become brothers and sisters." But really to become such depends upon our attitude of demonstrating our charity, of committing ourselves to others.

The sin of the Levite and the priest was not that they had no feeling of compassion. It is natural for everybody to have these feelings. Their sin was to avoid meeting the one in need, to put themselves in a situation of not having to commit themselves (". . . on seeing him he passed to the other side of the road and went on his way. . . ."[12]). This attitude prevented them from making themselves brothers (neighbors) of the wounded Jew.

The Samaritan was a brother to the wounded one, not by reason of his religion (the priest, the Levite, and the Jew had the same religion; the Samaritan was a heretic), nor by his race, nationality, or ideology (it was precisely he who was the only one who had nothing in common with the Jew), but rather by his charitable attitude.

My neighbor is not the one who shares my religion, my country, my family, or my ideas. My neighbor is that one to whom I am committed.

We become brothers and sisters when we commit ourselves to those who need us; we become more so when our commitment is more complete. The Samaritan was not content to give himself partially to the wounded man. He treated him, he bandaged him, he picked him up and carried him to an inn and paid for all that he needed.[13]

The giving of oneself in love is the measure of brotherhood. We are not brothers and sisters if we do not know how to be effectively compassionate to the end.

To approach the Jew, the Samaritan had to make an effort to come out of himself, to put aside any thought of his race, his religion, his prejudices. ". . . One must know that the Jews do not communicate with the Samaritans. . . ."[14] He had to put his own world and his own immediate interests aside. He abandoned his travel plans and gave of his time and money. As for the priest and the Levite, we don't know if they were better or worse than the Samaritan, but we do know that they never left their "own world." Their projects, which they did not want to upset by interrupting their journey, were more important to them than the challenge to become brothers to the wounded man. They considered their ritual and religious functions more important than fraternal charity.

To become a brother or sister to another presupposes leaving "our world" to enter "the world of the other," to enter his or her culture, mentality, needs, poverty. To make oneself a brother or sister presupposes, above all, entrance into the world of the poor. Brotherly love is so demanding and difficult because it consists not only in lending an outward service but in a gesture of service that obligates us, that pulls us out of ourselves to make us identify ourselves with the poverty of the other. Our world of riches, of knowledge, and of power, our lifestyles and the prejudices of a society that is divided into classes and unjust on all levels, separates us from the poor.

To make oneself brother to the other, insofar as the other is poor and needy, as a going out of my own world, takes on the qualities of a reconciliation. In treating the Jew as a neighbor, the Samaritan reconciles himself with him and in principle with those of his race. Each time that we make of the other our neighbor and brother in circumstances of conflict, of personal, communitarian, or social division, we become reconciled with him. That the rich man becomes a brother to the poor signifies that he does him justice, establishing the process of a social reconciliation. The same must be said of politicians separated by ideologies, or of races and nationalities that are at odds.

The idea of neighbor proclaimed by Jesus in his reply to the doctor of the Law leads to a universal brotherhood, to justice, and to reconciliation. To make ourselves neighbor to the poor and needy is the demand placed upon us by the interpretation Christ himself gives to the second commandment of the Law. This demand is for each one of us: "Go and do likewise."[15]

IV
Following Jesus in the Poor

"... Lord, when did we see you hungry and feed you or thirsty and gave you to drink, or stranger and welcome you, naked and clothe you, or sick or in prison and visit you?" "Truly I say to you as you did it to one of the least of my brothers, you did it to me."[1]

According to the parable of the Samaritan, my brother is revealed as the needy one, the poor one. In the parable of the Final Judgment,[2] Jesus confirms this teaching, and adds to it a decisive element: the brother, and particularly the poor person, is a representation of himself. He identifies himself with the poor. And so, Christianity comes to be the only religion where we find God in human beings, especially in the weakest of them.

There is no Christianity without this sense of brotherhood nor without a sense of the poor. The sense of the poor is essential to the message of Jesus, as essential as the sense of prayer. It gives to a sense of brotherhood its realism and its concreteness. On the other hand, the demand of a universal brotherhood avoids the possibility that the option for the poor, which is proper to the Gospel, become sectarian or classist. A sense of brotherhood and a sense of the poor are dialectically complementary demands.

31

Even more, for Jesus the commitment to our poor brothers and sisters is one of the decisive criteria for our salvation. "Ye blessed of my Father, come and inherit the kingdom. . . . For I was hungry and you gave me food". . . etc.[3]

The meaning of the poor in the Gospel goes beyond an ethical-humanistic predilection. It verifies the authenticity of our following of Christ.

Therefore in Catholic spirituality, this sense of the poor appears as inseparable from the meaning of God, so that a conversion to the Lord always implies as an important dimension a turning to the poor. (This does not exclude other dimensions equally important in Christian conversion.) This affirmation runs through all Catholic tradition and teaching. The idea already appears in the Prophets, particularly those of the Exile, that the very worship of God is in vain without justice and mercy toward the needy; that the conversion that God wants expresses itself in the service of others, especially of the oppressed.[4] The church offers us an abundance of prophetic texts in the readings of Advent and Lent in order to dispose us for a really true conversion.

The preaching of Jesus reinforced this teaching, making the following of him consistant with his call to dedicate ourselves to the liberating service of the poor in whom he becomes mysteriously present. Hence the poor are declared blessed and their evangelization and human liberation is a privileged sign that salvation is present among us. "He sent me to preach the good news to the poor, to proclaim liberty to the captives, and to return sight to the blind; to set at liberty the oppressed and to proclaim the Lord's year of grace. . . . Today this prophecy is fulfilled. . . ."[5] "Go and tell John what you have seen and heard: the blind see, the lame walk, the lepers are cleansed, the deaf hear, the dead rise, the good news is announced to the poor."[6]

And the church, throughout all its history, in its most authoritative and constant teaching, has always and everywhere inspired in its children a sense of the poor as an essential part of the Christian life. It is possible that at certain times and places this teaching was weakened in ordinary preaching, or that significant numbers of Christians did not live according to this teaching, or that it was presented only in a spiritual dimension without considering the social consequences. . . . But it is undeniable that this has always been the most official teaching of the church. And the saints always understood this to be so. The saint, that follower of Christ with whom the church identifies itself and whom the church presents to us as a model of discipleship, is a person who always combines with a deep sense of God a keen sense of the poor and of service to them.

FOLLOWING THE POOR JESUS

The novelty of the Gospel message with respect to poverty does not end here. Jesus does not only ask us to have a sense of the poor brother or sister, with whom he identified. Jesus also asks that we ourselves become poor, that we follow him in his condition as a poor person. Blessedness is not only a call to feel with the poor; it is a challenge to us to become poor ourselves. We find ourselves confronted with the demand of evangelical poverty, an essential element in the following of Jesus.

The following of the poor Christ is a radical freeing of the heart: detachment from situations, persons, and things in order to grow in love, which is the conversion to "the other" and to community for Jesus' sake.

The blessedness of poverty sets free in love. As with every Christian attitude, it is saturated in love, and in this case poverty is a condition of love. The freedom it produces is at the service of a dynamic charity which tends to become more and more universal and limitless. It would not be possible to love the way Jesus wants us to love without truly having a poor heart. If obedience is the measure of love and chastity its sign, poverty is its prerequisite.

It is true that sociological poverty is not evangelical poverty, but both are existentially related. If we have the proper interior disposition, material poverty will normally be a help toward an interior, evangelical poverty. On the contrary, riches always entail a danger for our freedom of heart. It is also possible that there are sociologically poor whose reaction to things and to people might not be evangelical, and rich people who are poor in heart. But the harmony between the two "poverties" is evident. For this reason an authentic poverty of spirit always tends to express itself in a visible, material form. Anything else would be an illusion and would lack the necessary anthropological expression. In this sense every Christian who lives the blessedness of poverty must express this in some form of exterior detachment.

This interior poverty which expresses itself externally—and this we definitively call evangelical poverty—is not an evangelical counsel, as it has at times been presented. It is Christ's call to each Christian, a universal demand of Christianity. "No one can be my disciple if he does not renounce all that he possesses."[7] Each Christian must respond to this call constantly, every day, according to individual circumstances. This response is not a static one; it is in no way patterned. It will vary according to the type of function, culture, temperament, health, social circumstances. . . . But each Christian must be conscientiously seeking a personal way of responding to this demand of the Gospel. The call is universal; the response must be sought in each case in faith and in prayer.

Finally, the blessedness of poverty, visibly expressed

as a prophecy of the Gospel of hope, consists not only in a certain lack of or detachment from money or material goods. There are other elements of poverty much more profound and significant, that perhaps on the threshold of Christian life are not so obvious. At first only "material" poverty is stressed, but with the passage of time and as the life of faith matures we discover a very real and inherent dimension of a true poverty of spirit.

Detachment in the face of prestige, of criticism, of the various kinds of "power" and "advancement" are forms of poverty to which God calls the Christian—and especially the apostle—in the various stages of the path of mission. The "poor," in short, are not so much in opposition to these who "have" certain things as to the self-sufficient, the proud, those who have focused their interests outside the values of the kingdom.

JESUS AND RICHES

"No one can obey two masters, because he will hate the one and love the other, he will esteem the first and despise the second. It is impossible to serve God and money." [8]

The discourse of Jesus on the poor and poverty is incomplete if we do not take into account what he said about the rich and riches. For the Gospel delivers his proof to us in an unexpected way: Jesus in his discourse speaks much more often of wealth and the wealthy than of poverty and the poor.

One of the reasons for the ever contemporary relevance of the Gospel is the fact that it does not conform to the dominant tendencies of "public opinion" or of statistics. Paradoxically, it is also one of the reasons why it has had so little visible effect on the majority of the people.

The comments of Jesus on wealth and money are precisely in line with this. In times like these when ideologies that originated in capitalism or in Marxism give a privileged place to the economic sphere and make the problem of production and distribution of wealth the cornerstone of their historical success, the works of Jesus appear anachronistic and condemned to being admired but not imitated.

The recounting of the teachings of the Gospel on wealth and the wealthy do not present an optimistic balance. Jesus does not condemn money in itself. This is consistent with his approach; he condemns no thing: he condemns or forewarns against people's attitudes toward things. In the case of money or wealth, his warnings are so systematic that Christians are forced to examine all our "spontaneous" criteria and attitudes about the question.

For Jesus, the radical ambiguity of wealth consists in its tendency to become "lord" of the human heart.[9] This new "god" leaves room for no other. Either we serve the God who frees us or the god who by enriching us chains us to the earth. The option between Christ and money implies a vision of life and of the human vocation. To serve money is to both make a god out of the earth and to pervert the purpose of its goods and of the person who uses them. The warning of Christ in this respect is clear: "Do not lay up for yourselves treasures on earth" . . . they are precarious and futile . . . they pervert the heart and the reason for existence. . . . "For where your treasure is, there will your heart be also."[10]

That's why Jesus is so severe with the rich. His teaching on human liberation consists not only in declaring the poor blessed and privileged heirs of the kingdom. There is also a warning and a call to the rich. It even surprises us, in reading the Gospel, to note that Jesus addresses at least as many discourses to the rich as to the poor, discourses with a content equally liberating, though different.

For a rich man "it is more difficult to enter into the kingdom of God than for a camel to pass through the eye of a needle."[11] He who makes of riches "his consolation . . . shall hunger . . . and mourn and weep."[12] Before God, "he is pitiable, poor, blind, and naked and deserves compassion."[13]

In his discourse on riches, Jesus, for whom "all is possible,"[14] and who "came to seek and to save what was lost,"[15] has a redeeming intention. The rich man must change, ceasing to "store up things" for himself instead of becoming rich before God.[16] He must rediscover the deep significance of his riches and money according to Christ's criteria.

THE SIGN OF "THE FRUIT OF THE EARTH AND THE WORK OF HUMAN HANDS"

We are so immersed in the civilization of "having" that we no longer know the Christian meaning of money: to be a sign of the goods of this world, that God gave to us, so that we might develop them and distribute them among all people. Humankind invented money in order to make the transfer and distribution of these goods more feasible. In itself, it ought to be the means of giving to those who have nothing what others have in excess. Money should be at the service of justice, facilitating the redistribution and equality of wealth.

Actually, money becomes the great source of injustice and inequality. In becoming the "lord" of human beings, it acquires value by itself. It loses its meaning as a sign of the goods of the earth, of which all people, without exception, are owners. As an absolute value, money necessarily becomes a source of power, of human exploitation, of division.

The teaching of Jesus on providence and confidence in God presupposes that people respect the Christian idea of

wealth. When we betray this, we turn the word of Christ
into an illusion and a blasphemy.

Jesus' plea in the Lord's Prayer, "Give us this day our
daily bread,"[17] fails not because we lack God's love and
justice, since he has provided ample bread for all, but
rather because people are "slaves to riches," who pile
wealth up in the hands of just a few, "building ever larger
barns in which to store and preserve it,"[18] thus depriving
the poor.[19]

The promise of Jesus is absolutely sure—of "not being
preoccupied, wondering what we are going to eat in order
to go on living, or what we will wear . . . since the birds of
the heavens do not sow or reap, or gather into their barns,
and yet your heavenly Father feeds them. . . . How much
more will he do for us. . . . We are of more value than the
birds. . . . Therefore let us seek first the kingdom and his
justice and all these things will be added."[20] But this is
reduced to rhetoric when the sin of institutionalized injustice condemns millions of people to situations of misery
and insecurity far worse than the birds of the heavens.

Money is also a sign of human work, of the sweat of the
brow, of sacrifices, and even of blood. Capitalism per-
verts this meaning, giving primacy to profit and making
work subject to it. We can no longer relate money with the
noble and hard work of the *campesinos,* of the miners, of
the working class, or with the creative and exhausting
work of the intellectuals. Money has become dehumanized.

Money, sign of "the goods of the earth and of the work
of human hands," in Christ's perspective ought to be a
means of brotherhood and reconciliation between the rich
and the poor, a means of reestablishing the equality and
the justice destroyed by the exploitation of work and of
profit in a civilization that adores wealth.

For Christ, those who have more on this earth that is
God's and therefore belongs to everyone are nothing but

faithful and prudent servants . . . set over the household to give them food at the proper time.[21] Just as no one is absolute owner of the earth, so neither is anyone owner of money. This is always to be administered in the name of God, as is power and authority also.

This was the discovery made by Zaccheus, one of the rich men to whom Jesus spoke and who was converted. Upon reconciling himself with God and with the people whom he had exploited, Zaccheus shared his money with them as a sign of that reconciliation and restored brother-hood.[22]

The church has always understood that the fraternal reconciliation that it is called upon to create among people must lead them to share their riches and to recognize the work of those who have produced them. This conviction of the church has become a permanent teaching and at the same time a fervent prayer in the Eucharist, the source of all reconciliation.

In the Eucharist, the body and blood of Christ, given up to reconcile human beings with God and with one another, is offered under the symbols of bread and wine, which represent "the fruit of the earth and the work of human hands."[23]

For the church the eucharistic reconciliation presupposes that that reconciliation begins by doing justice to the goods of the earth and the work of human hands. This reconciliation in justice means that goods are distributed so that they reach and serve everyone, and so that work regains its dignity and primacy over profit.

"USE CURSED MONEY TO MAKE FRIENDS FOR YOURSELVES" (LUKE 16:9)

Is money in itself an inevitable source of iniquity, in spite of the eucharistic intercession of the church? Are riches evil, as it would appear from the words of Jesus and

from the attitude of many saints? For the Christian this is
the same as asking yourself about the conditions for the
redemption of money and of wealth. We believe in the
possibility of liberation of all reality, because of Christ
who took upon himself the whole human condition, not to
condemn it but to save it.[24]

Jesus not only condemned domination by money. In his
teaching we also notice the key to its redemption. This key
follows the same line as the liberation of power, since
money is one form of power and as such its use is not
legitimate unless it furthers God's plan of justice and
fraternity. Riches are redeemed when they are at the
service of the poor and the needy in concrete history.
Private, social, or international wealth becomes legitimate
when it is a means toward fraternal charity and social
freedom.

The rich who in the Gospel found favor with Jesus were
those who placed their wealth at the service of their
brothers and sisters in need. The typical case is Zaccheus,
as we have mentioned,[25] whose episode with Jesus was
definitely not just casually mentioned in the Gospel, but
rather serves as a model for the conversion of a wealthy
man.

The parable of the good Samaritan brings us the same
message. The charity of the Samaritan toward his fellow
human beings in need, which Jesus set forth as a model of
love of neighbor, contains many rich and complex les-
sons. In this parable we are commanded to overcome all
discrimination of peoples (Jews-Samaritans), to go from
compassion to action; to take upon ourselves all the sacrifices demanded by charity; to freely give of our resources to aid our oppressed brothers and sisters. The
Samaritan was a man of means (we do not know how
wealthy he was) which he used to help the wounded and
robbed man. "Take care of him, whatever else you spend
I will pay you when I return."[26]

Again, in the strange parable of the wise administrator,[27] Jesus shows us how a person with no financial scruples can always be saved if only the corrupt position of economic power is changed into one of service to the needy and exploited. Thus, "the cursed money" is redeemed and "we make friends for ourselves in the eternal habitations."[28]

MONEY IN THE SERVICE OF THE KINGDOM

The most dazzling case of the redemption of wealth is that of its use in the apostolate. The church, in carrying out its mission, uses money, and at times large amounts of it. Today this poses many serious questions about the institutional poverty of the church with regard to the possession and use of money. The extent, the challenges, and the complexity of evangelization in contemporary society have constantly increased the cost of the means of missionary activity. On the other hand, the wealth of the church keeps its radical ambiguity and its tendency to set itself up as the "lord" of the ecclesiastics, just as Christ foresaw in the Sermon on the Mount. Money can become a source of power, accumulation, and injustice in the Christian community. The wealth of the church also needs a constant redemption.

In its evangelical ideal, the church is radically poor. Its only wealth is Christ and the mission he commends to us. The church has no other possession than the apostolate and the necessary means to carry it out. Only thus can it justify the use of money; only an apostolate that is a ministry of reconciliation redeems the money of the church.

In the contemporary pastoral approach, the poverty of the church cannot simply be set forth in terms of "having" or "not having," but rather in other more profound and demanding terms. Neither can it be considered in terms of "economizing." To economize before the challenge of the kingdom of God is not always poverty. The criterion of "economizing" in the church can be, once again, accumulative. The apostolate is not at the service of money ("you cannot serve two masters") but the opposite. An evangelical and pastoral criterion for the use of money in the church is to ask oneself in the first place what is the good of the kingdom and what is the will of Christ and then spend what is necessary. Facing the glory of God and the good of others, to give with largesse is a form of poverty, since in the church money belongs to the Lord. This is the lesson Jesus taught to Judas Iscariot in the anointing at Bethany. Judas was scandalized by the "waste" of the ointment; he was concerned with a better "investment" of the money.[29]

What are the criteria we can use to reconcile the ideal of poverty with the use of money, at times great quantities, in the apostolate? To reconcile the possession of resources at the service of the kingdom with the need to redeem those riches?

The Christian community must face this problem as part of its fidelity to Christ in every place and in every age, without ever considering it resolved a priori. We must not act as if the problem of money in the apostolate does not exist; it must be recognized and solved evangelically.

Meanwhile the church will give witness, asking of the members of its communities, both rich and poor, as well as the local churches (where there are also rich and poor) what it asks of all humanity: to practice justice and to share "the goods of the earth and the works of human hands." The church will be an effective yeast of fraternity and reconciliation when its communities can offer to the world realistic models of fellowship in the goods of this world and a respect for poor and humble labor.

I also believe that the apostolate, even though it must

have recourse to money in order to extend itself, ought to possess an institutional style that gives witness to the Gospel power of "poor and simple means"; for the church is not simply a society that possesses and administers financial resources but the community that proclaims the beatitudes.

The witness of "poor and simple means" in the apostolate consists, in the first place, in living according to the Word that warns us that "we cannot serve two masters." The author of the apostolate is Christ himself, and all material resources ought to be relative to the strength and power of his grace. The church puts its confidence in Christ only, not in its material goods, and the church knows that the profound effect of evangelization goes far beyond the means of action used.

In concrete attitudes, in its criteria and decisions, the Christian community ought to give witness that, over and above any material resource, it puts confidence in the power of the word of the Gospel, in charity and in commitment to justice, in poverty, in prayer, and in the cross. The Christian community knows that all the rest will come in addition. This is the deepest way of expressing belief in the promise of Jesus: "Do not concern yourselves about riches; our Father knows what we need; before all else to seek the justice of the kingdom."[30]

This witness of "living poorly" in the apostolate prevents us from thinking that because there are no financial means "nothing can be done"; or thinking that money determines the efficacy of the mission. This attitude is not only evangelical but is borne out through pastoral experience, at least in Latin America: very often the poorest dioceses and churches are the most dynamic, the most missionary, the most credible to the people, the most faithful to the Council and to the Medellín Conference. On the other hand, many apostolic works which in their beginnings were pastorally successful, constantly striving for a fidelity to Gospel values as regards poverty, decline and become corrupt as regards their original objectives when they become rich and develop their models of action in a material way.

The "poor way" in the use of the means of the apostolate also demands that these conform to the message being proclaimed and to the ambience in which it is carried out. If the means which are used in evangelization are in contradiction to its content—the beatitudes—and to the poor to whom it is presented, we are "rich" in our missionary method: we use "rich means" in relation to a certain message and people. The message becomes obscure and rhetorical; the people do not understand it and they feel that it is not meant for them.

The Gospel never fails. In the apostolate, methods may not be considered apart from the content; the means used to transmit the message greatly affect its credibility. We cannot preach the beatitudes convincingly using a style and method which belie them; we cannot address the poor with a style and method that are strange to them, and that place us in "the world of the rich."

The consequence of all this is that evangelization, whether of the rich or the poor, whether with more or fewer resources, if it is to bear lasting and deep fruit of liberation for the poor and of conversion for the rich, ought always to be done "from among the poor"— "from" not necessarily as "place" but as solidarity with and an option for the cause of justice, which in Latin America is the cause of the poor. This is what decisively determines "poor means," redeems the use of money in the apostolate, and makes credible for rich and poor every discourse on wealth preached by the church.

V

Following Jesus the Contemplative

---

*"If you knew the gift of God and who it is that is
saying to you 'Give me a drink,' you would have
asked him, and he would have given you living water.
. . . Whoever drinks of the water that I shall give him
will never thirst again; because the water that I shall
give him will become in him a spring of water welling
up to eternal life. . . ."*[1]

Following Jesus in his love for his brothers and sisters
and for the poor, even being ready to give our lives, is not
the result of our own strength or own will. To be faithful to
this following not just for a time or under an impulse of
youth or of enthusiasm but rather for our entire lives goes
beyond our possibilities. But "what is impossible for man
is possible for God."

This following of Jesus is revealed to us as a gift from
God: the gift that Christ offered to the Samaritan woman
at Jacob's well, which becomes in us a kind of inexhaustible water which will never allow us to thirst again,[2] which
makes us born again in the Spirit,[3] and which transforms
us from egoists into followers. To speak of following
Christ is to speak of disposing ourselves to receive and to
grow in this gift. It is to speak of the contemplative dimension of the Christian life and of the way of our prayer.

The gift of God comes to us in a special way in prayer, in which we put on Christ who fills us with his plenty. Prayer communicates to us the experience of Jesus. This contemplative experience is necessary if we are to remain faithful to the demands of following him. Even more, prayer is an integral part of this discipleship: to follow Jesus is to follow him also in his prayer and contemplation, in which he expressed his absolute intimacy with the Father and his complete giving of himself.

Prayer is also inseparable from following Jesus because of the motives that inspire it, because of its mystique. What gives quality to any commitment is the mystique that inspires it, or the motives for this commitment. If there aren't profound motivations and a stable mystique, the commitment will wither. This is particularly so in Christian spirituality, whose motivations do not come from pure human reason or from analyses and ideologies, but rather from the words of Jesus heard in faith. To have a personal experience of these words in our contemplative prayer is to nourish our mystique and to make of our motives for following these words a "source of living water." The mystique of our discipleship is inseparable from the experience of our prayer.

To address the question of whether prayer still has a place in today's world is not a bad idea. In theory and in practice many Christians doubt the efficacy and meaning of their prayer, in a culture that is becoming secularized, where statistics and technology foresee the near future more and more, where human beings are acquiring a growing responsibility for and dominion over nature and its laws. Moreover, in this context prayer can be seen as an evasion, an alienation.

To many it appears that prayer reinforces a dualism (encountering God in prayer vs. encountering God in the

service of human beings) which has already been overcome in today's world.

In the principles for a solution that we now propose, we
suppose that the way we pray changes, although it might
be a permanent value of our Christian life. It can be
formulated in a very different way, depending on the
cultures and the sensitivities of an era. We do not manage
to integrate our prayer with our lives because the way we
ought to pray today is different from the way in which we
were taught to do so. This has produced a crisis. We do not
know how to integrate prayer within the psychological
demands of our day.

In the first place, we know a very impressive fact: that
Christ, the perfect man and head of all humanity, prayed.
He prayed and made prayer one of the focal points of his
life. And Jesus—the same yesterday, today, and forever
—continues his life of prayer together with the Father
"always keenly interceding for us."[4] This prayer was and
is the salvation of humankind, and acts upon and influences what neither technology nor humanity can: sin,
liberty, faith, love, and redemption. By our prayer we
incorporate ourselves into this prayer of Christ and enter
in a real way into collaboration with him in the profound
salvation of humanity and of history. God desires our
collaboration with him, and in this perspective prayer—as
well as apostolic action—makes us enter fully into the
mission of Christ beyond human senses and power.

On the other hand, to come to a full understanding of
Christian prayer, it is necessary to be convinced that our
God is a personal God, one who listens, who communicates with us, with whom we can have a relationship, and
with whom we can become intimate, as we can with any
person. The God who is revealed to us in Jesus Christ is
not a first cause or a philosophical abstraction. He is a real

person, with intelligence and will, who has decided to enter our history, to bring us to participate in his life, to listen to us and to act in us. If we are convinced of all this, prayer is not a practice or a "ritual" but rather a response to the Christian vocation, a need of love and a proof that there is no true friendship and collaboration with a Person-God without constant dialogue and communication with him.

Humanity, by its very nature and through the seed planted in baptism, is called upon to meet God not only through mediations (neighbor, work, events, etc.). We can and must meet him as he is. To contemplate God, Truth and Goodness, as he is, is a value that we cannot renounce.

There is, therefore, historically in humanity an innate vocation to contemplate God face to face (contemplative vocation). If we do not attain to this we will always be incomplete human beings. With difficulty will we be able to meet Christ in others. And prayer is essentially the response to this vocation of humanity; it is the only activity that unites us to God "face to face," with no mediations, except the darkness of faith. The manner in which we meet God in prayer is on a different level than that of other encounters (neighbor, etc.) and we cannot refuse it without diminishing our own development and destiny. At the same time, prayer is our guarantee that we will really discover Christ in our neighbor and in history, and that we are not just left with good desires.

The ability to find Christ in others does not come from our own psychological effort but rather from a grace that comes forth from our own conscience, the fruit of faith nourished by prayer, that gives us the experience of Christ at its source.

Christian prayer, therefore, is on another level than that of statistics, psychology, or technical advancement. It is not in competition with them, nor is it endangered by humanity's progress, just as God and liberty or progress are not excluded. This is so as long as prayer is authentic, that is, an expression of a personal love for God and others. At the end of our days we shall be judged by our love (not so much by prayer . . .), but prayer is precisely a special proof of our love for God and leads us equally to love all others, inevitably if it is authentic. The alternative between prayer and the service of others is false; it supposes a "prayer" that is not Christian, that is alienated with no reference to the world and the rest of humankind. Prayer is not a refuge in God that separates us from our commitment to others; it is an ever-growing prompting that reveals to us that this person that we meet in prayer we ought also to meet in others.

And the prayer of petition? Does it make sense when human beings can control the laws of nature? We have already said that Christian prayer makes us partakers in the prayer of a Christ who prays unceasingly for the conversion and the development of humankind. And this prayer is the only thing that can influence what humanity possesses of transcendence over any law or progress: freedom. We pray and petition because we know that only God can change freedom without obliterating it, and that the great personal and historical decisions depend on humanity's freedom. In the apostolate, to be concrete, prayer extends beyond the limits of action. Experience itself shows us that all our zeal and organization come up against a reality which we cannot change: human freedom. It is there that faith reveals to us our possibility of changing that freedom into collaborating with God, in order to save, to convert, to bring peace, to come to decisions that make for justice and fraternity.

From all that has been said we see that prayer is not at the level of the empirical, it is not a psychological or

sentimental necessity. It is a conviction of faith. This very
truth implies the difficulties that we meet in praying or in
truly believing in prayer. Its effects—social, apostolic, or
psychological—are not seen immediately. They are
realized over long periods of time, profoundly, tied to
decisions of human freedom and the course of history. So
God has desired to associate us with his providence so that
we may collaborate in the making of history not only by
our actions but also by our prayers.

From this we see the need of basing our prayer on firm
convictions, rooted in Christian faith. On the other hand,
if our need for prayer is merely psychological or sentimental, we will easily abandon its practice for any activity or
thing of greater or lesser importance. Habitually, the
problem of "lack of time" to pray is related to this.

Finally, and now from the point of view of life, and of
Christian life and the apostolate, we know that there are
certain evangelical demands—especially in the realm of
heroic charity, of generosity—and the cross, of fidelity to
our mission beyond all disenchantment—before which we
need "superhuman" graces, a very special presence of
Christ. Now then, there are graces and there are experiences of Christ in our lives that God gives us only during
prayer. It is here, in an encounter with Jesus the Person
renewed each day, that we develop a oneness with God to
see things, to judge, to act, and to love in accordance with
the Gospel. The lack of necessary prayer in our lives, if it
is culpable and habitual, leads us into a sort of spiritual and
apostolic anemia with the accompanying powerlessness
to be faithful to all the demands of the Gospel.

Another characteristic of Christian prayer is based on
the fact that it is an answer to God's initiative, a God who
speaks. It is not humanity who takes the initiative in
prayer; it is God who has spoken to us first, who has called
us in the course of life, a call to which human beings

respond with their attitudes of prayer. Christianity is not a religion like the others, in which human beings seek God and satisfy in their religious lives a natural need of a relationship with their Creator. Christianity is, above all, a religion of a God who seeks out human beings, a God who takes the initiative to love them, to redeem them, and to form with himself a unity in charity.

The liturgy, the teacher of prayer, by its very structure, embodies this mystery of call and response. In the liturgy, prayer (songs, silences, common prayers, etc.) usually comes after the proclamation of the word; it is a response of human beings who have just heard the word of God spoken to them. This structure of the liturgy reveals the entire profound meaning of Christian prayer.

This prayer, which must be a response to God in Christ, takes on a historical and incarnational character which is also characteristic of Christianity. If one had to make a phenomenological distinction between the prayer of a Buddhist and that of a Christian, the distinction would have to be made on the level of history and of the Incarnation. The dialogue of Christians with their God forms part of a personal and collective history, which can be situated in time and related to experiences and events.

For this reason Christian prayer is said to have its own anthropology. It takes into account the specific, historical, incarnate human being, with a body, with an existence and a being capable of understanding words and signs. This anthropological element of Christian prayer has often been forgotten by pastors, not only in liturgical prayer but also in private prayer. In order that prayer take into consideration the whole person who relates to God, we cannot underrate the postures, the bodily attitudes, the intelligibility and the affective value of religious signs, of vocal expressions, of the texts that nourish prayer. . . . All this, which is essential to the liturgy, should not be forgotten either in the teaching and development of personal prayer.

Therefore the problem of our prayer is very much related to our way of life. There are lifestyles, with no control or personal discipline, psychologically incompatible with activities demanded of us in the exercise of our faith, such as prayer. If such discipline does not exist we will not have the freedom we need for an authentically contemplative encounter with God.

We need discipline in our lives. A minimum of self-control is indispensable in order to be faithful to prayer and its human laws.

Another important element in this anthropology is method. There has been great insistence on methods of prayer ever since the sixteenth century. We are not referring here to the rigidity of certain traditional methods but rather to the personal way of aiding our faculties to concentrate on God. We must not forget this if we do not want to multiply unnecessarily the practical difficulties and distractions in prayer.

Our distractions should not affect us. What is important is the efficacy of the work of the Holy Spirit in us. Distractions have to do with the affective part of our nature, and during times of distraction many things come to mind which help us to know ourselves better. In these moments the profound motives of our subconscious come to light as well as the people and things that concern us. We have to give all of this to the Lord; it forms part of the sincerity of our prayer.

All Christian prayer has an ecclesial dimension. That is to say, a Christian never really prays alone, even in the most private moments of prayer. The Christian always prays as part of a whole, which is the church, always in union with all humankind, and always in a certain sense "with the church."

Finally, we must say that the reflections that we have

made regarding the nature of prayer lead us to redefine the authentic contemplative Christian.

Contemplation is not the traditional image we had. It is not fidelity to practices of prayer. The practices are only a means; they do not constitute contemplation of faith.

The contemplative today is the one who has an experience of God, who is capable of meeting God in history, in politics, in our brothers or sisters, and most fully through prayer.

In the future you will no longer be able to be a Christian without being a contemplative and you cannot be a contemplative without having an experience of Christ and his kingdom in history. In this sense, Christian contemplation will guarantee the survival of faith in a secularized or politicized world of the future.

VI

Contemplation and Commitment

---

*Then the virtuous will say to him in reply, "Lord,
when did we see you a stranger and make you welcome; naked and clothe you; sick or in prison and go
to see you?" And the King will answer, "I tell you
solemnly, insofar as you did this to one of the least of
these brothers of mine, you did it to me."* [1]

One of the most important tasks of the church in Latin
America is to reformulate the great themes of faith and of a
validly traditional spirituality, in terms meaningful for the
type of commitment that Christians assume today. This
commitment is more and more socio-political and in many
cases strongly conscious of participation in the liberation
of the poor and the oppressed.

In this task, the theme of contemplation in relation to
liberation and its demands of commitment appears of
prime importance. This synthesis between the "militant"
and the contemplative is urgent in order that the faith of
Latin Americans today not become alienated from their
lives and from the history that they are called upon to live
and in order that it not, in the worst of cases, even disap-
pear. This is so much more necessary now because of the
misunderstanding created in the last thirty years among
the various "types of spirituality" of Christians.

The last two decades have seen two types of "Christian lifestyle." They could be described as the "religious contemplatives" and the "committed militants." The first are very sensitive to the values that are properly speaking "religious": to prayer and its practice, to the liturgy and the sacraments, to the transcendent dimensions of Christianity. They are, or were, less sensitive to the temporal or social dimensions.

The second group emphasizes more their commitment to historical tasks, social militancy, the "praxis" of liberation, in the sense of an integral, evangelical liberation that implies the overthrow of social, economic, and political subservience. To a certain extent they mistrust the sacramental life, prayer, and, in general, Christian contemplation. One important reason for this, of special interest to us, is the ambiguity in the doctrine and in the facts of the "traditional" concept of contemplation.

In fact, ever since the earliest centuries, contemplation, and above all contemplative prayer, had two different aspects. There was the Greek-platonic aspect, with similarities to the oriental mysticism of Buddhism, Hinduism, and Islam. It was known for its individualistic character ("man alone, face to face with his God"), its strong sense of the transcendent and orientation away from life and its events. For this reason it easily became withdrawal. This platonic-oriental mysticism corrupted to a greater or lesser degree authentic Christian mysticism, not as an isolated incident, but rather to the extent that Greek thought and "ethos," above all with its dualism, influenced the infant church. Along with this influence there was the tradition of genuine biblical contemplation, contemplation that we could call "historical" or "committed." It is precisely this aspect of Christian contemplation which we ought to revive in all its fullness today.

THE EXPERIENCE OF CHRISTIANS

What is so interesting as a major ecclesial reality in Latin America is that this revival is actually taking place in the experience of many Christians and groups of Christians, above all in those committed to different options related to liberation.

In these, many Christians are seeing themselves as participants with the Lord in redemptive tasks that are part of the building up of the kingdom. Many are growing even more as they dedicate themselves to socio-political commitments. From a tendency to question their faith and even to lose it, they now tend to strengthen it, to recover prayer, and to rediscover its meaning.

To illustrate this experience we adduce the testimony of three Christians, very dedicated to socio-political works. For them their option for "liberation" is the Christian option, with no historical alternative, although they do admit different political partisan alternatives. Their Christian training did not prepare them for this, and yet they discovered a great affinity between their choice and their faith.

These Christians react against an ahistoric salvation. They want salvation to be effective, to be joined to temporal and political commitments, even though they do not reduce salvation to politics or to just a temporal liberation.

These Christians place great emphasis on commitment, on praxis. They see in it a decisive point in the Christian dimension of their lives: precisely the values that demand this praxis, this commitment. They discover in prayer a way of assuring the presence of these Gospel values in their action. Even beyond this, they have recovered the true meaning of prayer and of Christian contemplation through their very commitment to liberation.

"In the social struggle, in working toward liberation, the danger is that 'the others' become, in practice, the enemy. This can happen very quickly if there are no 'moral' values," says one of these Christians. "Therefore it is necessary that there be an irruption of the transcendent, of the Gospel, in the personal life of the believer. Prayer brings this about. Otherwise, one becomes merely a pragmatist, without values, or assumes the ethics of Marxism-Leninism. We might even fall below the nonbeliever."

"Prayer in my experience," asserts another, "in no way neutralizes the power of a commitment to liberation. On the contrary, it gives us the ability to find a more fraternal, more human, more 'civilized' way to effect this liberation."

"Prayer really identifies us, in the light of our own consciences, as Christians, for it avoids dualism: dualism between faith and action, which has led many of our companions to lose their sense of faith. Prayer is the 'bridge' between a commitment to liberation and our convictions as believers."

"The person, the Christian," asserts another, "must experience here and now in his or her commitment both the kingdom and hope. We must not become discouraged. We need consolations beyond our immediate experiences, which are often deceiving. Personal and contemplative prayer assure this type of experience."

"Christians committed to liberation are contemplatives insofar as they capture what God desires for 'the other' and make of this the heart of their commitment. They are contemplatives, as I see it, because of their capacity to maintain the universal character of charity, without giving up their preference for the oppressed. Even beyond this, they are capable of developing forms of nonpartisan solidarity with the poor. . . ."

THE CONTEMPLATIVE SOURCE OF COMMITMENT

These experiences are not just intuitions without Christian value. They are a reference, "a theological locus," insofar as they respond to the rediscovery of the authentic concept of contemplation. This is not just prayer, even though prayer is an indispensable and privileged form of contemplation, a very intense moment in our life of faith.

Contemplation is related to the vigor of faith and the capacity of this faith to shed new light on life and history. Contemplation means to experience God really, even though obscurely, in every phase of human life. It is the capacity to meet Christ and the experience of having met him through a vigorous and incarnate faith: "What we have seen and heard, what our hands have touched concerning the word of life . . ."[2] (the contemplative witness of St. John). Such faith is always found in the contemplative.

This "experiential encounter" with God—who reveals himself to us in Christ—presupposes the two contemplative encounters given us in the Gospel. The first is that of the very person of Jesus. The New Testament presents this encounter to us as the root of every conversion of faith and of the contemplative life. The revelation of Christ to the people of his time (Zaccheus, the Samaritan woman, Peter, the disciples of Emmaus, etc., etc.) created in them an encounter and a contemplative experience. Each of them is a type of Christian, and to be a Christian and a contemplative is the same thing in the New Testament. This same contemplative encounter was experienced by the apostles, already mature in the experience of 1 John 1:1. It appears unique to the apostolic vocation in the Transfiguration.[3] This episode responds to the discovery of a new dimension of Jesus by the three disciples, a contemplative dimension that goes beyond action. ("It is good for us to be here. . . . Let us make three tents. . . .") The encounter with the person of Jesus has for the apostles a value in itself; it is privileged and at this moment surpasses the experience of the action.

St. Peter had the same kind of contemplative encounter[4] and such is the experience of all the saints.

The second encounter is inseparable from and complementary to the encounter with the person of Christ. It is the experience, again contemplative, of the presence of Christ in our brothers and sisters, above all in the "little ones." This is typified in the famous pericope: "I was hungry . . . and you gave me to eat; . . . as you did it to one of the least of these my brethren, you did it to me."[5] Here the encounter with the suffering and needy brothers and sisters (the "little ones") and the resultant service is an experience of Christ—as contemplative, therefore, as a personal encounter with the Lord.

Both encounters are inseparable. The first underlines the fact that Christianity transcends any temporal reality; the second that it is incarnate and inseparable from the love of neighbor. The first reminds us of the first commandment, to love God above all things, and of the absolute value of the person of Jesus. The second recalls the commandment that is like the first, to love our neighbor as ourselves and the presence of Christ in this love.

The first encounter gives rise to contemplative prayer and the various ways of relating to God; the second to a temporal commitment as a contemplative experience. The second encounter "incarnates" the first and gives a historical dimension to the encounter with God and to our life of prayer.

The experience of Jesus in the service of our brothers

and sisters also gives a whole social dimension to Christian consciousness, thus transcending any purely individualistic and private consciousness as well as any contemplation with "platonic" tendencies. It gives to fraternal love a social and collective dimension insofar as the
"little ones" are, in Latin America, not only individual
persons, but also—and above all—human groupings,
neglected subcultures, social classes, or sectors. . . .
There is in them a collective presence of Jesus, the experience of which is truly a contemplative act.

Contemplation thus conceived gives a socio-political
content to the faith, and faith itself acquires a historico-
social dimension without reducing itself to just this. The
Christ encountered and contemplated in prayer "continues" in the encounter with the brothers and sisters, and
if we are able to experience Christ in service given to "the
little ones" it is because we have met him in contemplative
prayer. Contemplation is not only the discovery of the
presence of Jesus in the neighbors ("you did it unto me")
but also a call to action in their favor, a commitment to
liberation ("what you did"). The contemplation of Christ
in the suffering and oppressed is a call to commitment. It is
the historical content of Christian contemplation in the
Latin American church.

The encounter-service of the poor is contemplative in
those who have faith and makes them "contemplatives in
action" in the best Christian tradition. This is not an
automatic experience; it comes about to the extent that
the Christ encountered in prayer emerges in the Christian
conscience, as a background for action. "The Other"
experienced in contemplative prayer is experienced in our
encounter with "the others." Neither is this an improvisa-
tion. It presupposes prayer, which is activated in service
to others, thus acquiring a social content.

Dedication to my neighbors and to their liberation, on

the other hand, insofar as it is contemplative, implies an accompanying and marginal presence of the Christ encountered in prayer. This marginal consciousness of Christ is the point of union between prayer and commitment, and it prevents the latter from becoming empty by including both in the contemplative experience. Christian mysticism is a mysticism of commitment.

REFORMULATING CHRISTIAN CONTEMPLATION IN LATIN AMERICAN TERMS

These reflections give rise to the necessity of reformulation or of completion of the concept of contemplation, while maintaining its traditional values.

The essence of real Christian prayer always consists in "going out of oneself in order to meet the Other." In contrast with an attitude that might appear as egoism or as an evasion of reality and responsibilities, true prayer is a supreme act of abnegation and forgetfulness of self in order to meet Christ and his demands in others. In this sense prayer is related to the classic themes of death, and the cross—"death to self in order to live for God"[6]— which implies the crucifixion of egoism. That is why Christian mysticism goes through the purifying "dark night of the senses,"[7] through loneliness and aridity, which causes egosim to die and leads us out of ourselves in order to find the Other. We touch upon this theme of "the desert" as an essential element of Christian contemplation.

The desert in the Christian tradition is, above all, an attitude of the spirit. But many of the great contemplatives, including Jesus,[8] St. Paul,[9] many prophets,[10] the early monks, many contemplative orders, and Charles de Foucauld in modern times, went into the geographic desert often during their lives to sense this spirit with the help of an external sign. The geographic desert is symbolic of an attitude of clearance, of putting oneself in a situation of truth, with no illusions before God, of a radical poverty that makes us expect all as a gift from Christ, of silence in which we can listen to the word of the "Other."

The desert symbolizes the attitude of human powerlessness before salvation. It is to be ready, in the painful experience of our limitations, to receive this salvation through no merit of our own, with the obscure conviction that God is seeking us and that Christianity, more than the love of humankind for God, is the love of Jesus, who first seeks out humankind.

These great fundamental themes of Christian contemplation have been set forth with an almost exclusive reference to God. They are in the line of the "first encounter" of the New Testament referred to above, which relates us contemplatively with the person of Jesus. We believe this description is incomplete and that it is influenced with characteristics of Greek-oriental mysticism. To recover the authentic concept of Christian contemplation, in a meaningful form for the faithful committed to the cause of liberation, we must extend these same themes to the "second encounter," to the contemplation of Christ in our neighbor, in the little one.

So, in order to find Jesus in "the other," in order to discover "the other" as "other" to whom I must give myself and not as an extension of myself and my interests, I need to go out of myself, to die, to crucify selfishness. To the extent that we die in order to live for God, we die in order to live for our neighbor and vice versa.

And this capacity to live for our neighbors, especially if they are poor and the least of people, is the decisive source of the temporal commitment of the Christian, and of the socio-political dimension of charity and of contemplative faith. It is the basis of the public and social dimension of

Christian contemplation, which up to now has been unduly private. There, and not in a revolutionary dialectic, do believers find the strength of their militancy and of their work of liberation.

The same desert attitude, that of contemplation, is united to this commitment. If the contemplative-desert forged the great prophets, then present-day Christian prophecy in Latin America equally needs the contemplative attitude of the desert. The attitude of "going out of one's self," to come face to face again with the absolute and with the true meaning of things, allows one to "leave the system" as an unjust and deceitful society, in order to denounce it and to free oneself from it. If Christianity does not "go to the desert" in order to get away from the "system" it will never be free or prophetic and able to liberate others. If it does not learn how to be silent in itself in order to silence the "oppressors' words" and to listen to the word of the truth that makes us free, in the attitude of "the desert," Christianity will not be able to transform its world prophetically or politically. Contemplation which frees one from egoism and from "the system" is the source of freedom and of the capacity to set others free.

Authentic Christian contemplation, which crosses through the desert, transforms contemplatives into prophets and heroes of commitment. Christianity brings about the synthesis of the militant and the mystic, of the politician and the contemplative, overcoming the false contradiction between the "contemplative-religious" and the "committed-militant." Authentic contemplation, which through the encounter with "the absolute of God" leads to "the absolute of the neighbor," is the meeting place of this difficult symbiosis, so necessary and life-giving for Latin American Christians committed to the liberation of the poor.

THE BIBLICAL MESSAGE
OF CONTEMPLATION AND COMMITMENT

The current Christian proofs of the contemplation-commitment synthesis and the recovery of its authentic content are rooted, of course, in the best tradition of Christianity and the Bible. The prophets, Elijah above all, appear to take this line: guides of a people, critics of a system, proclaimers of a message of liberation, not from a power position but rather from the people and in their service and from a contemplation of the word of God which impels them to action. This is the mystical-political line of the militant Christian that springs from the people and from the word and not from power.

In this contemplative line we must situate the figure of Moses as a symbol. It is typical of the politico-mystic that he had a very deep experience of God in the desert, and without ceasing to be influenced by this experience he led a people toward their freedom. Service in the liberation of people through their participation in power is a very likely definition of a Christian politician today.

In this enterprise the contemplative quality of Moses led him to come face to face with the absoluteness of "the other" in the solitude of the burning bush, and with the absoluteness of "the others," in whom his experienced faith led him to discover a people among whom God dwells and to whom he had to announce the freedom of the children of God. This contemplative quality also allowed this mystic not to be discouraged by this people who often showed themselves as mediocre and to accept, therefore, the loneliness of his prophetic leadership. ("Why does Yahweh bring us to this land . . . would it not be better to return to Egypt? . . . Let us choose a leader and go back. . . ." "Why have they taken us out of Egypt to bring us to this awful place . . . ?")[11]

In this prophetic solitude, Moses, notwithstanding, remains firm in hope "as if he could see the invisible." Because of his contemplative faith "he considered the humiliation of Christ more precious than the riches of Egypt."[12]

This hope, which belongs to "political prophecy," sustained Moses even to the ultimate sacrifice in his mission: at the end he himself did not enter into the promised land to which he had led his people. He sacrificed "power" to help in the "liberation of his people," faithful to his contemplative grace.

The case of Jesus is also profoundly enlightening, although in a different way. His contemplation leads to a commitment which is not directly temporal but rather pastoral-prophetic. It had socio-political consequences more proper to the ministry of evangelization than to temporal-political action.

The commitment of the contemplative to the poor and the little ones can be seen under two aspects. The first is the directly political option. In this Christians channel their charity—serving Christ in the "other"—through the mediation of projects of change and political means that will help to effect these projects; to do this they must participate in power. They strengthen their partisan option, because they see that this is the best way of effecting liberation. Here their contemplative commitment becomes strategy and partisan politics.

The second way of commitment to the "little ones" is that of the prophetic option. In this, charity, source of contemplation, is channeled into the effective and operative proclamation of Christ's message concerning the liberation of the poor and the "little ones." This message leads to the formation of a critical consciousness and is capable of bringing about liberating transformations that are deep and decisive. In this sense it has socio-political consequences. This option is less common and therefore more charismatic.

A committed love needs both of these expressions, which are not always exclusive one of the other, just as human love expresses itself in marriage and also in the more prophetic and less common form of celibacy. Both forms of loving are intense, as both forms of militancy which we have noted are efficacious and legitimately Christian. The second form, more proper to the pastoral ministry and to the hierarchy—although it does not absolutely exclude other forms of commitment—is the form of militancy adopted by Christ himself and the apostles. With this they renounced power and political partisanship, but created instead the consciousness necessary for progressive liberation from all forms of oppression.

In making known the presence of God in every human being, and thus the dignity and absolute destiny of all human beings, Christ and the apostles not only made known their own contemplative vision of humanity. They also gave a socio-political content to this prophetic proclamation by making it incompatible with the prevalent social system and pagan attitudes toward human beings.

In giving a privileged status to the poor and needy and identifying himself with them in a special way, Christ summoned and mobilized the poor for the kingdom of God. This is not only a contemplative action—the presence of Jesus in the dispossessed and the intuition of their dignity. It also led to social commitment with political consequences, for the incorporation of the poor into the kingdom of God takes place in history and implies a progressive liberation of these poor and needy from concrete social systems.

Jesus proclaimed the beatitudes. It is impossible to announce and to live this message without living in hope, without being a contemplative. But the beatitudes themselves are the "ethical attitude" of contemplatives. This radical living out of the Gospel is a prophecy that invariably challenges individuals and societies.

Thus the biblical message from Moses to Jesus gives us both views of the contemplative commitment to liberation. In the mystique of Moses, liberation takes on a temporal and political face and prefigures the total liberation in Christ.

In the mystique of Jesus this full sense is present. Liberation takes on an eschatological and decisive face, saving and transforming both humanity and society from within. This implies socio-political changes just as the liberation of Moses implied hope in the unknown and the eschatological vocation of Israel.

Both symbols have a contemplative message. All Christians in Latin America today live these to a greater or lesser degree in different ways—always complementarily, according to their function or vocation. They unite mysticism and commitment in the same contemplative call because the source of their Christian vision is the same: the experience of encountering Jesus in prayer and in our neighbor, above all in "the little ones."[13]

VII

Following Jesus
Faithfully Even to the Cross

*Jesus arrived with them at a place called Geth-
semane. He said to his disciples: "Sit down here
while I go inside to pray." . . . And he began to feel
sorrow and anguish. And he said to them: "I am
sorrowful unto death." . . . And prostrating himself
face down upon the ground he prayed: "Father, if it
is possible let this chalice pass from me. However,
not my will but thine be done."*[1]

Christian spirituality finds in Jesus not only a model of
discipleship but also a way to be faithful to this discipleship. Jesus was faithful, absolutely faithful to the mission
given to him by his Father; he chose to be faithful;[2] he was
"complete love and fidelity."[3] To follow Jesus in his
fidelity to the Father is the peak of Christianity.

Jesus' fidelity developed in the midst of history, of
concrete circumstances, in a society and among people
like those of today, marked by deceit and sin. That's why
Jesus' fidelity is painful and full of conflict: he had to bear
the burden of sin and the force of evil of those who opposed him. This opposition was so strong that it brought
about the apparent failure of his public life and rushed him

into death on the cross. The cross is the sign of the ever ruling power of evil, of sin, of injustice in the world. It is also the supreme proof of the fidelity of Jesus. His cross —and ours—has no meaning except that contained in fidelity to a mission. That's why we have said that, properly speaking, there is no "spirituality of the cross" but rather a spirituality of fidelity and discipleship.

This helps us to understand the Christian cross from the point of view of following Jesus and his cause. Jesus crucified taught his disciples and all generations a new way to suffer and to die, through fidelity to a cause.

THE LIBERATING MEANING OF THE CROSS

But the cross has a particular significance for the suffering, the oppressed, for those resigned to their fate. For them, the message of crucifixion is that Jesus teaches us to suffer and to die in a new way; not as if we were beaten down or despised but in fidelity to a cause full of hope. "He who does not take up his cross and follow me, cannot be my disciple,"[4] says Jesus. It is not enough to carry the cross: the Christian difference is to carry it as Christ did (to follow him). "Take up the cross" is not then a stoic acceptance or resignation but rather the attitude of one who carries commitment to the full extent. "No one has greater love than he who lays down his life for his friends. . . ." "Jesus, having loved his own, loved them to the very end."[5]

This is the new manner of carrying the cross that Christ teaches us with his death: transforming it into a sign and source of love and dedication, for a liberation that is always incomplete but guaranteed through the promise.

The absolute novelty of the tragic, historical destiny of Jesus is the promise it contains, a promise that will see its complete fulfillment in the resurrection and exaltation with the Father. If the cross is an apparent frustration of a promise, the height of abjection for Jesus and the failure of his mission, paradoxically, it is at the same time the moment of the beginning of his triumph.

The oppressed and the suffering, of all human and social categories, will tend to project onto the Crucified One their own frustration. The cross would be the failure of the cause of the just, of the oppressed, and of those who fight for justice, the failure of the beatitudes. The cross of Jesus is that of the forsaken; it appears that the "little ones" and the weak ones cannot triumph.

But if the martyrdom of Christ is precisely the moment in which the Father takes up his cause, giving to him forever the full freedom of his exaltation and placing in his hands the freedom of all people, then the failure of the abandoned ones of this world is only an illusion.

In the cross of Christ, the Father takes to himself and reconciles those who suffer abandonment and desperation as the supreme form of impotence and oppression. He gives them the gift of suffering not as a conquered people but as actors committed to a cause, which is the very cause of Christ. The identification of the oppressed with the cross is not their identification with the humiliation of Christ but with his resurrected power, which calls them to a certain task. It has nothing to do with "overcoming the cross" but of making of this cross a power to effect the liberation of themselves and of others.

If the message of the cross is that we can suffer and even die in a new way, it is because of this hope that it brings to us. If we have been brought to the crucifixion, we have in the crucified God the firm promise that the power of the resurrection will never allow those who suffer and die for justice' sake to be defeated forever.

The cross is the sign that the cause of the just and of the oppressed, which appears to have been frustrated, has already been accepted by the Father. Therefore they have not been abandoned but that they ought to give themselves even more fully to bringing about the reign of justice, following the footsteps of a Christ crucified but never completely overcome.

In Jesus the cross is his own mission of the liberation of human beings turned into a tragedy because of the sin of these very same human beings, but full of the power to recreate this mission in a new transfigured way. The cross of the oppressed, of the suffering and the abandoned, goes to the very heart of their own unjust situation. And the cross is found in the resultant process of their liberation, ruined apparently by egoism and sin, but with the power of thrusting itself ahead continually in a way that is always new.

THE EXPERIENCE OF THE FIDELITY OF JESUS

The fidelity of Jesus is the model of our own fidelity. The fidelity of Jesus was demonstrated in the historical context of the human experience of his commitment to the cause of the Father. Following Jesus does not mean to repeat the historical forms of his fidelity (which cannot be repeated) but to redeem the experience of our own fidelity, taking to ourselves the experiences of the fidelity of Christ through faith and love. The prophetic mission of Jesus was made up of the contingencies and trials of our own mission, and in the prophetic experience of the Son of God we find the inspiration of our sense of being prophets: to be faithful to the Father's cause in the web of our history. Contemplation of the prophetic journey of the Lord can help us in this.

At the beginning of his mission, Jesus enjoyed moments of popular prestige, of social influence, even of power. On beginning his activity "announcing the good news to the

poor, liberty to the captives, light to the blind, freedom for
the oppressed and reconciliation to all,"[6] Jesus responds
to the messianic expectations of the people. He wants to
manifest through signs his liberating power and he devotes
himself to healing the sick, the lepers, and the tormented.
He multiplies the loaves, provides wine for the feasts. The
people seek him out, they crowd around him; it is sufficient for them to touch his robe to be restored to health.[7]
He doesn't even have time to eat[8] and in order to pray he
has to go off to isolated places at night.[9]

It is the time of his great discourses to the multitudes. In
order to make himself heard he has to go up to the hill-
tops[10] or into the boats.[11]

Tens of thousands follow him.[12] His visibility and prestige are at their height: Jesus seems to respond, as the
greatest of the prophets, to the aspirations of the people
. . . although "he did not fully trust himself to the people,
because he himself knew what was in man."[13]

At this point they wanted to make him king.[14] For him
this moment is the return of the temptation in the desert,
for the devil had left him "to return at the opportune
time."[15] The temptation that recurs from time to time
during Jesus' ministry consists basically of institutionaliz-
ing his earthly prestige at the cost of the model of fidelity
given him by the Father. Jesus rejects this[16] and, aware of
the ambiguity of the image that his ministry gave to the
people, he decides to destroy this misunderstanding by
radicalizing the demands upon his followers, knowing of
the crisis this would mean for the people and his mission.
"You seek me not because you saw signs but because you
ate your fill of the loaves. Do not labor for the food that
perishes, but for another food which endures and gives
eternal life, which the Son of Man will give to you."[17] And
he speaks to them of faith, faith in his word, and in his
body as food, as conditions for following him and arriving
at true life and true liberation.

The people are not prepared for this. They had other expectations: there is a massive disappointment. Jesus is openly criticized[18] and becomes a controversial figure and a source of conflict.[19] Even some of his closest followers leave him.[20] And for Jesus, now surrounded by just a few, a new stage of his life begins, the stage of "impoverishment." He is argued about, misunderstood; something has been lost which originally seemed necessary for his activity: popularity. With this the most decisive experience of his life begins, the real poverty of the "Servant of Yahweh." Now he scarcely performs any miracles and for some time he stays away from the crowds. His discourses undergo a notable change with his new experience. He speaks less of messianic expectations and of the power of the kingdom and more of discipleship and of the cross that he must bear. He announces his Passion, the persecutions and the death that he senses close at hand.

For the Son of God this is not just a "pastoral strategy." It is the fruit of the experiences of "impoverishment," of rejection, of persecution, that have accumulated in the way of his life not only through the crisis brought on in the people by the demands he made for following him but rather by his now obvious conflict with the authorities. "He did not want to go back to Judea because the Jews were determined to kill him."[21]

Jesus goes into self-exile because his hour had not yet come. But the die was cast. From the very first moment of his ministry in which, faithful to the will of his Father, he had proclaimed the true God and had placed the imperial authority and the Jewish religious theocracy in question, Jesus is subversive for a power that wants to be divine and blasphemous for a religious class that proposes a god of law and of observance.

The conflict that Jesus has created is fundamentally religious, but there is always latent a tension with the civil authority. (The massacre by Herod, in his infancy, which necessitates the flight into Egypt; the situation created by the execution of John the Baptist; etc. This tension will come to a head during his last stay in Jerusalem.) His persecutors are primarily the chief priests and the doctors of the law. This religious theocracy at first tries to discredit him; later they decide to give him up to the "foreigners," to the Roman authorities, as the only way of eliminating him.[22] From then on Jesus is a fugitive in his own country.

Misunderstood by many, rejected and persecuted by the ruling class, Jesus through these experiences is prepared for the cross. They are the signs by which the Father shows him that his hour has come. Jesus then makes his decision to return to Jerusalem, to the final confrontation. His apostles also have a presentiment of the outcome of this,[23] and they are afraid.[24]

At this moment, nevertheless, the people show their solidarity with him. Although they are not always capable of following him, they do recognize in him the Holy One of God, who preached a kingdom of brotherhood and justice where the "last shall be first" and the most abandoned are the privileged ones. They knew that this was the reason for his being rejected and persecuted by the alliance of the leading religious and political groups. That's why on his arrival in Jerusalem a large crowd acclaims him and follows him, and the whole city is stirred.[25] And the leaders fear the people.[26] In order to be able to defame and condemn him before the people, they decide to accuse him before Pilate for political reasons.

The solidarity of the people around him revives in Jesus the temptation of the desert: the possibility of a messiahship based on power and not on prophecy. The temptation becomes stronger and more dramatic than ever. Oppressed by this, Jesus on his last night goes apart to the Garden of the Olives to pray to the Father and to renew his fidelity to his will. At the same time, the anguishing experience of the persistence of evil and the power of sin, which at that moment seemed to have triumphed, reaches its greatest intensity. The crisis is so severe that the Son of God enters into his agony and his sweat becomes as blood.[27]

After this, there is the crucial experience of death in the abandonment of the cross. The fidelity of Jesus has been tested to the extreme and his resurrection is proof that it was not in vain: from then on, those who follow him to the sacrifice of the cross can transform this experience into a source of liberation and of holiness.

VIII

The Radicalism of Following Jesus

"I will follow you, Lord, but let me first say farewell to those at my home. . . ." Jesus said to him: "No one who puts his hand to the plow and looks back is fit for the kingdom of God." [1]

The word "radical" is a suspicious word. And even more so today because of its political connotations. A radical is an extremist, a foolish one, an imprudent person, the opposite of well balanced.

This is not so in Christian spirituality. In line with the following of Christ, the Christian must be radical, and, on the other hand, a certain "balance" could be ambiguous.

In the language of the Gospel, a radical is one who goes to the root of things, one who accepts the teachings of Jesus with all their consequences.

In this sense it is the inevitable condition for following Christ, and purely human "balance" can easily lead to mediocrity and lukewarmness. Real evangelical balance implies the radicalism of a commitment to Christ, and for this reason it cannot be identified with the "good judgment" and "prudence" of wise and clear thinkers, according to the pure categories of profane activity. The word of Jesus rejects this kind of balance and subjects it to Christian radicalism.

In the Book of Revelation, we read of the reproach of the false balance of the one who, under the guise of an honorable exterior mode of behavior, has lost radical love;[2] it also denounces the lukewarmness hidden under the false balance of accommodation ("Oh that you were either cold or hot . . .").[3]

In Christian terms, Jesus was a radical. He set forth in new terms the idea of conversion to God, the change in our life, and ethical and religious attitudes, establishing his Gospel as the only absolute. This is how it was perceived by the governing and priestly class as well as by his disciples. For many of his relatives this was a symptom of madness.[4] His radicalism cost him his life.

Jesus was radical in his demands. For him the Christian must be salt, and if the salt loses its ability to give savour to others it is no longer good for anything.[5] The Christian commitment must be like a light capable of illuminating the world.[6]

The choice for Christ must be a radical one. It occupies first place, above parents, children, and life itself.[7] Every good, every value must be sacrificed when it becomes incompatible with the radicalism of this choice,[8] like the one who sells all he has to acquire a pearl of great price or a hidden treasure.[9] Christ wishes to establish himself as humanity's only absolute commitment, doing away with this false balance of "serving two masters."[10]

Jesus demands a total discipleship, carried to the ultimate consequences. The gate leading to his kingdom is not wide or "reasonable in size" but narrow.[11] Those who follow him must be ready not to have a place to lay down their heads; they must be ready to do away with worldly attachments, and once on their way they should not so much as look back.[12] All earthly gain is as nothing if it separates us from him.[13]

Jesus does not hide the violence that one must do to

oneself in order to follow him[14] on a road that is necessarily marked by the cross.[15] The demands of Christ are such
that they ask people "to be born anew,"[16] that "they
become as little children,"[17] and that they "occupy the
lowest place,"[18] after having "lost and crushed their lives
like the grain of wheat."[19]

Christian radicalism, without seeking it, can lead to
conflicts and tensions, fruit of the reaction that absolute
fidelity to the Gospel causes. Because of Christ, the Christian will be an object of hatred[20] and division,[21] a sign of
contradiction.[22] Jesus himself was an object of hatred and
divisions, and before him it is impossible to maintain the
false prudence of indecision since one is either for him or
against him.[23] "I have come to provoke a crisis in the
world: those who do not see will see, and those who see
will become blind."[24] "Blessed are those who on meeting
me take no offense at me."[25]

The radical crisis of the Gospel of Jesus is summed up in
his ideal of happiness as opposed to false happiness, according to the beatitudes of Saint Luke.[26] In contrast with
the different categories of good judgment of a worldly
"balance," the rich, the satisfied, and the "preferred
ones" are disqualified by Jesus. On the other hand those
who for him are in the line of evangelical balance are the
poor, the hungry, the suffering, the exiled, the insulted,
and those badly thought of because of their Christian
choice.[27]

Jesus shows the same lack of "moderation" in the face
of certain specifically evangelical demands. The fraternal
love that he asks for is not only a "sensible" and "decent"
attitude of good feelings and human relations. For him we
are no different from the "pagans" who follow that ethic
of relationships, if we are not able to pardon offenses
"seventy times seven,"[28] if we don't learn how not to
judge another[29] and to love and pardon our enemies and

those who persecute us.[30] The radicalism of Christian love knows no bounds,[31] it demands no recompense,[32] leads us to love everyone without discrimination of any kind;[33] and even more than this, it demands that we choose for the weak and the "little ones."[34]

The faith that Jesus demands in his person and in his word is a radical one. It is not the faith of the "wise and prudent."[35] It ought to make us capable of superhuman undertakings.[36] It would be enough to have "a grain of that faith to move mountains."[37] Therefore the Gospel demands an absolute confidence in prayer, as an expression of the radicalism of faith.[38]

Jesus also sets himself aside from this "human balance" by setting forth the Christian attitude toward worldly goods, wealth, prestige, and temporal well-being. His idea of poverty is radical: "You cannot be my disciple if you do not renounce all that you have."[39] He commands us to seek above all the values of the kingdom, and all else depends on them.[40] Equally radical is his criticism of wealth[41] and of the various comfortable versions of the apostolic life.[42] The circumstances of his birth in Bethlehem[43] and of his identification with the insignificant and controversial town of Nazareth[44] are, in this same vein, options that call into question many present-day criteria.

Facing the truth, Jesus is equally absolute.[45] His fidelity to this truth brings him to the final confrontation with the authorities and with death.[46] In commiting himself to the cause of truth, Jesus will be radical in his criticism of hypocrisy, of outward appearances,[47] and of every kind of phariseeism.[48]

In its criteria of truth, the Gospel departs once again from the criteria of "worldly balance." Those who are last shall be first and those who occupy the first places in this world will be last.[49] Thus, prostitutes will enter the kingdom of heaven before many "respectable people,"[50] the faith of sinners is of more value than the religion that is only external,[51] the poor widow's mite has more value than the gifts of the wealthy,[52] and the repentance of the sinful publican justifies more than the self-assurance of the practicing pharisee.[53] According to these evangelical criteria even the apparently useless contemplation of Mary has more value than the productivity of Martha.[54]

The radicalism of the Gospel has its greatest incarnation in Jesus' giving of his life for all humankind.[55] Thus the cross remains as the unquestionable sign of radical commitment, of absolute fidelity to the Father,[56] of love carried to its extreme,[57] of seeking out the last place,[58] of the renunciation of power and of violence.[59]

THE SAINT AS RADICAL

The radical nature of the discipleship of Christ is shown equally by the testimony of those who have most authentically identified themselves with the evangelical ideal: the saints. For Christianity the saint is the incarnation of the ideal often proclaimed but rarely lived. Within the symbolic and profoundly human nature of Catholicism, the saint is the symbol of the evangelical ideal made visible and placed within the reach of all at a specific moment and in the face of specific challenges of history. The saint is the living commentary on the written Gospel, the Gospel proclaimed by the life of a person in all its radicalism.

This identification of saints with the Gospel demands that they go to the root of Christianity, leading them to the imitation of the historical Jesus as he is made known to us by the faith of the church, and to fidelity to his evangelical teaching without "accommodations." The church thus has two ways of identifying an authentic Christianity: through doctrinal propositions it guarantees revealed truth (orthodoxy); by setting forth the saints it guarantees the truth of Christian practice (orthopraxis). The lives of the saints incarnate what the magisterium proposes as true Christianity.

The saint is a radical witness, and the church demonstrates its understanding of this when it requires for canonization evidence that this person has practiced the demands of the Gospel "to a heroic degree." This heroic degree radicalizes Christian commitment, divorcing completely from any "middle way" or any purely human accommodation that looks at Christian heroism as "extremist," "exaggeration," or "radicalism" (falling once again into the ambiguity of transferring socio-political categories into a Christian commitment).

In matters marginal to its essential mission, the church can appear "restrained" and "politically well-balanced" (handling of questions of government, assumption of certain secular positions, etc.). But it is radical when it comes to identifying Christian authenticity. The church does not identify it with any forms of the "worldly balance" of its representatives. It identifies it with the radical heroism of the saints.

THE RADICALISM OF CONSECRATED LIFE

The Christian commitment to which the church gives rise also has another way of making its radical dynamism known: in the way it understands and carries out the consecrated life. The consecrated life, as a prophetic mode of living Christianity according to certain radically assumed values, is presented by the church itself as a privileged witness to the evangelical life. Thus, its characteristics and prophetic significance we can consider as authentically representative of the following of Christ.

We make no attempt here to exhaust the prophetic

dimension or the content of ecclesial witness of the consecrated life. What concerns us now is that we want to call attention to one characteristic aspect: its critical impact as witness to Christian radicalism.

We believe that it is appropriate to the religious life to call into question or even protest against the church and society: against the church, to the extent that it is decadent or ambiguous, or has lost its radical dynamism; against society, to the extent that it becomes dehumanized or dechristianized, and thus the source of oppression and injustice.

From the beginning, in the first centuries, we see such Christian protest. The radical ways of separating themselves from society and from the existing ecclesiastical structures (already influenced by post-Constantine decadence) proper to the first anchorites and primitive monasticism are a silent protest. This was an attempt to affirm dialectically (and often in a startling way, in the form of a break with ''the establishment'') Gospel values and intuitions that had entered into a process of comforming to the world and of mediocrity. The radicalism of their lifestyle raised many questions.

This characteristic continues to be typical of the great charismatic activities and reforms going on in the consecrated life. They imply a holy criticism of the society and the church in which they live. If, for example, we take St. Francis and his religious movement as a typical case, no one can deny that the radical Franciscan lifestyle implied a profound questioning of the worldly, clerical church of its time, and of the lifestyle of the feudalistic lords and of the emerging Christian bourgeoisie.

There is a tendency for all religious movements to lose the radicalism that was theirs at the time of their beginnings. The religious life becomes part of the ''establishment''; it takes on ''conventional'' ecclesiastical forms and above all the current lifestyles of society without questioning them. Such a case represents a partial decadence. A religious movement will never be authentic unless it returns to the root of its own prophetism. Its radicalism is a sign of vitality and of its right to continued existence. Its absence is a void that calls into question its very reason for existence in the church and in society. One of the causes of the present crisis in religious life rests on the fact that many who have given themselves to this life have discovered this void.

Authentic religious life implies a holy criticism of an established church: to the extent that Christians are no longer salt or light. It will criticize an "established" clergy—that is, established in obvious or subtle forms of "ecclesiastical careers." It will criticize ways of acting according to "political" or "diplomatic" criteria rather than evangelical values, in accommodation to "the world" in questions of power and of resources. It will criticize a clergy that tends to replace radical Christianity by the "balance" of the "golden mean" of the "respectable people."

Perhaps this last point is the most radical of the religious ideals as a typical form of discipleship. Christian balance is not the golden mean of the prevalent secular ethic. Christian balance is not "the middle of the road" but rather the truth as understood in the Gospel. The truth of Jesus is not always "in the middle"; often it is at the extremes, it is radical to an "established" criterion. At its deepest level, it is precisely this to which the consecrated life wishes to give testimony: the radicalism of discipleship in the face of the mediocrity of certain "golden means."

The consecrated life is also a radical criticism of society, a lifestyle that breaks with prevailing non-evangelical ways of thinking. In our concrete case in Latin America this criticism is of the injustices of a dependent capitalistic society. In other areas the consecrated life will call into question other vices of other types of society.

The consecrated life criticizes society not through "playing politics" or through critical socio-economic analysis. It criticizes it prophetically, taking on a way of life and organization that in itself is a reproach to the evils and practical non-Christian criteria of today's society. The consecrated ones are not radicals in the sociological but rather the evangelical sense. Their criticism springs from poverty and not from social activism: poverty as a rejection of a consumeristic mentality; as nonconcern for profit; as a fraternal way of sharing of material and spiritual goods; as a rejection of all forms of acceptation of persons and subtly "classist" categories, thus avoiding disguised ways of using others; as a commitment to the liberation of the "little ones."

In short, the consecrated life gives witness to contemplation, as a compendium of protest against the purely material goals of specific societies, capitalistic as well as socialistic. Prayer and contemplative experience are the greatest questions that the consecrated life directs toward society today. By valuing and exhibiting this contemplative dimension publicly, which is proper to evangelical radicalism, the consecrated life proclaims prophetically what is part of every Christian commitment: the absoluteness of God, gratuitousness, and the love of God above all things.

In fact, today social protest through radical lifestyle is not confined to the consecrated life or to other forms of Christian commitment. Different groups, above all those of young people, who adopt a counterculture (hippies and others) are basically a secularized caricature of Christian radicalism. In peaceful and at times also in violent ways, the current countercultural groups challenge society.

Their ambiguities, which are also great (tendencies to sectarianism, vice, and evasion of socio-political commitments . . .) are due to the fact that this secularized prophesy has not been nourished explicitly by the Gospel. However, they remain as a challenge to the current conformism of many forms of evangelical life. The latter is called upon to take up the social protest of the countercultures with a radically Christian motivation. This would allow us to move beyond the ambiguities of the countercultures and give to their lifestyle a truly prophetic meaning.

IX

Following Jesus Who Makes Us Free

"You will be my true disciple if you keep my word; then you will know the truth and the truth will make you free." [1]

As a lifetime process, following Christ leads us to Christian freedom. The freedom that Jesus brought to the world also takes place within us; liberation is an exodus from our servitude, enslavement, and sins. Therefore freedom of spirit belongs to the evangelical way and it coincides with the maturity of discipleship.

Freedom is a quality in people that they acquire through a growth process that continues throughout their entire lives. Therefore to be mature implies that one is also free and implies also a constant self-improvement. The problem is how to grow, how to continue acquiring that maturity in life. Our growth as Christians is conditioned by humanism, is tempered by psychology, and is founded in love. We continue to grow through love. Basically, Christianity is the re-ordering of our values in the light of love. Love is the crux of our life and what makes our freedom develop.

We must grow and become mature in all aspects, not only in one. We must be mature not only in age, experience, and intelligence. We must be mature affectively, socially, sexually, in our faith. . . .

86

There are many physically mature people and normally they give evidence of an intellectual maturity as well. But they are not always socially or affectively mature. The difficulties lie not in intellectual but rather in affective maturity.

We know that in human beings the first phase of maturity occurs in the sexual order and then possibly in the intellectual order. After this comes the phase of affective maturity, that is to say, the capacity to be objective about things, to separate oneself from situations and to look at them from outside. This is the capacity to communicate and to give oneself without always needing to receive something in return. We know that this is not easy and at times it will possibly take our whole lives to get to this point.

The same holds true for social maturity. This can be considered as the capacity to be oneself in any group. There are people who are mature in many ways, but socially they are not mature, that is to say, when they enter a group or have to face other persons, they stop being themselves. This is revealed by an excess of timidity, of aggression, of criticism, or through a tendency to contradict everything that the group says. Basically we are faced with people whose personalities have not been normally integrated. Social maturity presupposes the ability to integrate oneself into any group without our feeling greater or less than we are: with our assets and defects, with whatever we have to offer, with whatever we cannot offer. This presupposes having had some experience in life and having arrived at a knowledge of one's own self.

It is not enough to be free or to have attained maturity in one aspect. It is necessary to be mature in every aspect, because if one is not free in a certain area, it might well be enough to diminish and affect one's entire personality.

Such is the case of those who suffer liver trouble. It is just one aspect of our health but it affects the entire sys-

tem, especially as it touches on human relations. Our
growth should be harmonious, bound up in love, which is
the "lubricant" of a permanent growth.

Maturity does not take place on the ruins of our tendencies, although in fact this was how some have been taught.
We have these tendencies and they are good; they are part
of our character. It's not a question of destroying them but
of organizing them around love so that they may serve our
personal vocation.

It seems much simpler, for example, to cultivate chastity by doing away with contact with women, or with men.
The point is that true chastity is cultivated through the
integration of men and women into our lives. And this is
true freedom, true maturity.

Having made these general reflections, how could we
characterize maturity in our lives? How do we probe
ourselves more profoundly in order to see the measure or
the conditions of our freedom?

● In the first place, free, mature people are they who
live by convictions. There is a consistency in these people
between their values and an interiorization of them. The
values are integrated and consistent. Basically, immaturity consists in saying one thing and doing another. When
this becomes serious, we are facing a neurosis. The more
people lack this integration, the more neurotic they are.

On the other hand, immaturity consists in an inconsis-
tency in our values, in their internalization and assimila-
tion with reference to action.

● Mature, free people know their capacities and limitations. They are realistic with themselves, live by the truth,
know what they can and cannot do. Therefore they know
how to say no and also have the courage to say yes.

The more we have the courage to say yes or no the freer
we are and the more valid our commitment. For this
reason there cannot be a valid commitment where there is

immaturity. This holds true also in commitments made to God.

In working with adolescents one realizes that you cannot count much on commitments that they make, which is typical of adolescence. This, however, becomes serious in a mature person.

• Equally a sign of maturity and freedom is the capacity to put aside values incompatible with personal vocation. We are constantly putting aside incompatible values. Some people have committed themselves, for example, to celibacy at one point in their lives. But this implies the renunciation of matrimony, which is a value. To do this knowingly, consciously, without turning back, is a sign of maturity and freedom.

Immature people, on the other hand, want to have all good things at the same time. They choose one and then leave it to take up another, without setting any definite goals for themselves. Mature people know that matrimony is a value and that celibacy is also a value, but they choose one or the other according to personal choice, in a definitive way.

The capacity to choose alternatives, but without conflicts, without anxieties, is a sign of maturity and of freedom.

• Mature, free people are able to become part of a group without feeling that the norms of that group are a threat to their personalities.

This is a very important characteristic of the church: there are people who belong to a diocese, a community, or a congregation with which they are not in accord on everything. This puts them in a state of constant crisis and gives them the sensation of being attacked and overwhelmed. This is immaturity.

Free people live in any institution in which they have valid motives for remaining, even though they may not

agree with many things. They know that no institution is
perfect, whether civil or religious. But they do not feel
overpowered by it, because they have the ability to live in
ambiguous and provisional situations.

Today the church is living in an era of great transition in
its pastoral activity, in its religious life, etc. At times it
appears ambiguous. Those who do not have a sense of
personal fulfillment ought not to blame the church but
rather their lack of freedom and of maturity that does not
allow them to put up with ambiguous situations.

This also implies the capacity to live in tense situations.
We live constantly in this reality—in our pastoral work, in
the parish, wherever we find ourselves. There can also be
moments of tension with another person, with a group,
with a directive that doesn't satisfy us. . . . And the
capacity to live in these ambiguous and tense situations,
without giving up one's own values and ideas, but also
without breaking with the rest, is a sign of freedom, of
maturity.

All of us are called, with different rhythms, to this
maturity, to this freedom. The process will depend on the
fidelity and the events in the life of each of us. Evidently
the ones who have had a more difficult life, with tensions,
ambiguities, diverse experiences in different groups, the
ones who have had to free themselves from themselves in
order to become more integrated, will possibly arrive at
this maturity before others.

But in any case, God does not force us along this way.
We are the ones who must accept the rhythm of our own
growth, that growth toward which God calls us.

We must understand that this growth does not come
about without crisis. The crises in our lives are the conditions that make us free and mature. We must pass through
a series of stages in life. In each stage we create a synthesis
of our values. Crisis is nothing more than the transition
from one stage to another.

For example, we had made a synthesis of our religious life in the novitiate and the years that followed. After this we developed religiously. We have more experience and we arrive at a situation where this synthesis doesn't help us now; we see that it was insufficient and we have to make another, superior synthesis. While we do away with the former and build a new synthesis, we are in a period of crisis.

We can see that crisis is fundamentally the transition between two syntheses. And the more it costs us to make this new synthesis, the greater the crisis will be. We have a pedogogical problem. We do not have the right to destroy other people's syntheses if we do not give them a better one. We run the risk of leaving them in a permanent state of crisis for which there will be no solution. An unsolved crisis is a complete break with and the definitive abandonment of something of value.

We cannot grow without constantly remaking our own synthesis in the different stages of our life. A complete stability in our lives, never calling anything into question, if what we learned in the novitiate we keep as a permanent value—this is very suspiciously immature. Without doubt, what we have here is a Christian life that is not developing. In order to arrive at the freedom of maturity one must be ready to accept many crises.

Apparently the opposite can also occur, but the people who claim that they have never experienced a crisis are suspected of having lived a life of childishness and immaturity. When we hear of religious who have never had a crisis, who have been extremely stable in their community, "good" people who have never questioned anything, we see that they are not free, because they have never passed through the stages that lead to freedom.

In a meeting in which a bishop with an extremely free attitude participated, a psychologist said to me: "This bishop must have gone through many crises to have be-

come so free.'' Really, when we see people who are free
and who live in a responsible way, we know that it is
because they have gone through a number of breaks with
the past and through a series of crises of which at times we
have no idea.

Why these breaks and these crises to reach freedom?
Because all of us live more or less as slaves: slaves of false
values. We think that we live values, but in reality we live
ambiguities. Our lives are full of ambiguous values and we
must purify them so that they can become evangelical.

That's why crisis leads to freedom by revealing to us the
ambiguity of the values by which we live. At times it may
take years for us to become aware of this.

Some examples. Obedience is a value in religious life.
But there is a type of obedience without liberty, without
growth, without responsibility, and without fidelity to
one's own personal calling. Now this type of obedience is
not Christian because no Christian value, including obedience, should sacrifice or diminish other legitimate values
that are compatible with it. If obedience is truly a value,
then it presupposes that it will not violate freedom, responsibility, and initiative. When it does, it becomes an
ambiguous obedience.

A religious can say: ''I have been a religious for twenty
years and have never had a problem with obedience,'' but
this person could be living a very infantile kind of obedience and therefore not be free. Normally, any healthy
Christian nature, any healthy religious ought to have certain difficulties with obedience at different times of life. If
not, they are not developing. And they ought to be constantly remaking their synthesis and rediscovering this
same evangelical obedience, but each time with a new and
freer dimension. The ones who do not do this are at a
standstill. They will never ''bother'' anyone, because
they have never become free people.

Normally the people of greatest character, most maturity, are those who have the greatest difficulties with obedience. This is quite normal. One does not arrive at a free obedience without passing through rebellions. Obedience consists of a synthesis between the acceptance of the will of God and a complete Christian freedom. It is extremely difficult. It is a work of the Holy Spirit. And one does not arrive at this without having passed through many crises and even through many errors.

Prayer. There are persons who experience a certain ambiguity in the practice of prayer. They can go on for years indulging in prayer and in certain devotions without ever having arrived at maturity or at having developed an authentic prayer life. In order that there might be a true prayer, a free and mature prayer, it is also necessary that there be freedom as regards practice. And to have this habitually, people must pass through many crises without pressure. And the crises come about, for example, when they go out of themselves, change their life styles. This is the providential moment to become free, seeing the same values in a new light. It is the moment of purification of motives, without letting go what is worthwhile in prayer.

Freedom comes from an inner conviction, because of the Gospel, and it presupposes fidelity. But one does not arrive at this without going through a crisis and situations of transition, through which values are recovered in a completely different context. If we are not capable of doing this we are not growing. We remain mediocre, because it can be shown that many of the values by which we believe we are living are ambiguous and, quite possibly, not as pure as we think. And the way in which this ambiguity is revealed is through a crisis that will point us toward the truth and an evaluation of our life. That is why Jesus said: "The truth will make you free." Truth puts before us the stark reality and shows us that what we thought we were doing very well was actually no more than enslavement.

Another application of this is chastity. There exists a certain type of chastity that is not at all free: therefore it is not Christian. Often this is the fruit of a monosexual formation or of other aberrations. It is evident that people formed in an environment that consists only of men or of women can never have a normal development when it comes to chastity or celibacy. Later they will suffer the consequences, because you cannot do away with any tendency. The important thing is to receive formation in chastity and celibacy within a normal life pattern according to God's plan, that is to say, in the relation of man and woman. There must be an integration of both man and woman in the celibate Christian life. But this does not come about without crisis, without problems, without temptations. The normal thing is that there be crises and some problems in this aspect of our lives. It is the only way that Christian celibacy and chastity can be free. I can avoid crises, but I am definitely going to smother certain capacities of my personality that later are going to explode brutally as they seek compensation.

Now let us look at faith. It must become free and not be chained only to tradition, whether of the family, or of our educational system. We must face the option of having or not having faith, with the freedom needed so that it be truly mature faith.

The same can occur in pastoral activity itself. It can easily be that in an immature stage, the ambiguities of our human motives for prestige or competence may not be noticed. There is a failure to appreciate supernatural elements, an orientation not so much toward the building of the kingdom of Christ as of "our" kingdom. . . . From this comes impatience, discouragement, seeking after ecclesiastical favor, etc. This can in the end produce a crisis of a complete break and the ambiguity becomes apparent. Diverse circumstances and failures may lead to this. It is a moment to grow in maturity, to purify apostolic action, and to rediscover the depths of a Christian apostolate, to purify the value of pastoral work and to become truly free.

Therefore, if the values by which we live are ambiguous, conflicts are also necessary. Sometimes too (and this is delicate), conflicts will have to be raised. Because the only way that a person or a group grows is by going through crises and unmasking themselves in order to live with more and more freedom.

When a group is at a standstill, when there is nothing "new," when a person is at a standstill, there is a need to bring up these conflicts in a healthy, challenging way, so that there may be some progress. In the last analysis it means to choose our values anew, and with more and more freedom because, in reality, we have not yet chosen them with complete freedom. The choice was made with only partial freedom.

What is important in regard to prayer is that we choose it, without caring whether it is obligatory. It's always a question of choosing all our values, all our commitments, with more and more freedom, without thinking of what is demanded.

This presupposes the courage of facing the truth and the courage to be unmasked, because in our lives there are many lies that we unconsciously live, ambiguities that must be unmasked. Crises, conflicts, and doubts are events which, if we are sensitive to them, will be of help to us in this.

This is one of the benefits of the *revisión de vida.**

*"review of life," an analysis or evaluation of our actions in the light of the Gospel.

Starting with something concrete, with certain facts, it permits dialogue through concrete specific reactions. It allows us to change, casting light on our deeds and attitudes. I question myself to dispel my ambiguities.

In this *revisión de vida* we are not going to formulate principles for ourselves or recall doctrines. This we already know. There's no need to recall in theory the Gospel values. We ought rather to aid ourselves in questioning our own lives, so that we may see in our consciences what has been ambiguous and deceptive in our activities, and so nothing has universal significance in our lives. I ought not to enslave myself exclusively to any action. The day that I become a slave to an attitude, that day I will lose the possibility of growth. Even if I am only thirty years old or less, I will lose my youth. I will be fixed in a certain way of thinking and of acting. This is why we must examine our problems with courage and constantly call ourselves into question.

There are those who believe that time will take care of everything, because they do not have the courage to open themselves to conflicts. Time often makes things worse. To leave things to time may occasionally be the wisest thing to do, but other times we must be aware that problems are worsening because we don't have the courage to face them and to expose them to the truth which will make us free. We must never try to avoid crises artificially. Nor, on the contrary, should we provoke crises in others without there being a good probability that this person is ready to face them and to grow.

X

Jesus and the Liberation of His People

The Spirit of the Lord has been given to me;
for he has anointed me.
He has sent me to bring the good news to the poor,
to proclaim liberty to captives
and to the blind new sight,
to set the downtrodden free,
to proclaim the Lord's year of favor. [1]

Many Christians today are committed to the integral liberation of their brothers and sisters, particularly of the "little ones," those who suffer all kinds of injustice and other kinds of sin which characterize Latin American society. In many instances these Christians are in no condition to assume a militancy that is in itself political. In other cases this militancy is either not advisable or it is functionally—not doctrinally—incompatible with another mission. This is the case of the hierarchy of the church and in general of those dedicated to the official pastoral ministry.

For these and for many other Christians there remain the demands of liberating the "little ones" from all types of injustice and sin if they truly follow Christ and his

Gospel. They realize that they must influence society in favor of the poor through their apostolic mission; that as Christians, their action should have a socio-political dimension; and that in this, as in other aspects of the apostolate, Christ and the Gospel are their model.

However, many of them seem to find themselves today at an impasse. They appear lost in the maze of a socio-political pastoral approach, and do not find their inspiration and orientation in the Gospel. That is to say, they do not see Jesus as a model in this field. In other aspects of life, Jesus and his Gospel orient them with words and deeds. In the attitude of Christ in regard to the social and political problems of his time they find a vacuum, or a complete abstention that leaves them in the dark. Or they would like to see in Jesus a definite option regarding the demands of the social liberation of the Jewish people and against the Roman system, in the style of a militant, a revolutionary, a contemporary political prophet. And in this field, Jesus' life doesn't seem to give them any message that can be imitated. From all this arise two temptations: that of a purely "religious" apostolate with no reference to social change, or that of replacing Christ with other persons apparently more committed to the historic liberation of the oppressed.

THE PROBLEM OF A "POLITICAL CHRISTOLOGY"

It seems to me that this is a real problem in Latin America, and its cause is the absence of a Christology that responds to this uneasiness, a Christology with social and political dimensions. The Christology that many of those Christians received did not prepare them for a socio-political reading of the life of Christ and the Gospel. To grasp the liberating and temporal dimension of the words and deeds of Jesus, it is necessary to integrate this Christological dimension. A Christology thus conceived and which, of course, does not forget all the other dimensions of Christ's message is going to be the foundation of everything else: of the problems having to do with the relations between the church, society, and politics and between pastoral activity, politics, and liberation; of questions proper to a spirituality of liberation; of a political theology and of a theology of liberation.

The lack of a correct reading of the Gospel leads to deformed views of Jesus' stand on the socio-political situation of Israel. This is not the place to go into detail on this situation, which is well known. The Jewish people, subjugated by the Roman authorities, was looking for its political and economic liberation from the oppression of Caesar's representatives and from various taxes. In the time of Jesus there were politico-religious movements for this purpose. The idea of authority as something *sacred* and of theocratic states united in these movements the political and the religious orders to a point of confusing them in the work of opposition to the Roman power. Of these factions, the ones particularly important for us are the Herodians, who allied with the Roman authority and who took advantage of the system. These would correspond to our present-day Latin American oligarchies. Then there were the Essenes, a sect of deep and intense religious life and organization who kept themselves free from temporal and political matters. Their attitude is similar to the Christian sects of today who steer clear of the socio-political dimensions of the faith.

The most significant group for our present discussion was of the Zealots. Very nationalistic, they actively sought independence through subversion. Religious, they were involved in the battles for liberation of Israel with messianic zeal. They awaited the Messiah as the political leader who would free them from the Romans. Their influ-

ence was great, and the background of many of Jesus'
disciples, and probably some of the Apostles, was Zealot:
("Do you want us to command that fire come down from
heaven to consume them?"[2] . . .). They would correspond to the present-day Latin American revolutionary
movements.

We must situate the mission of Jesus with regard to this
reality and this historical process. The absence of the
political dimension of Christology tends to divorce Jesus
from the problems of his day socially: disincarnate, a
preacher of a message of salvation for people and of a
kingdom that has nothing to do with this world. The concrete historical and socio-political situations are a
backdrop for and an occasion of Jesus' purely religious
activity, but they are not intrinsically bound up with it.
The events and the people in the Passion, for example,
would be like actors prepared beforehand by the heavenly
Father so that the Redemption could be carried out. This
perspective sees a strong influence of the Essenes on
Christ.

Moreover, this Christology gives birth to a vision of the
church and its mission with no reference to society and
with no political dimension. It encloses the pastoral ministry in this type of mission and any apparent breaking out of
this enclosure is judged as an undue intrusion by the
official representatives of the church. ("The priests are
getting involved in politics . . .")

Reacting against this ahistorical Christology and seeking in the life of Christ an inspirational model for the tasks
of socio-political liberation, others have seen in Jesus'
mission in Israel the work of a revolutionary messiah,
who, besides giving a religious message, put into motion a
form of political subversion. They consider him if not a
Zealot, at least someone closely connected to the Zealots.
This is how they would explain, in the last analysis, that

the motives for his being taken prisoner were of a political nature (wanting to be equal to Caesar, making himself king of the Jews, endangering the stability of society: "If we allow him to continue this way, everyone will believe in him and the Romans will come and destroy our holy place and our people."[3]) This is the Christology of the revolutionary Christ, the model of the struggle for the temporal liberation of the oppressed. This leads to an ecclesiology in which the church and its hierarchical ministers would be called upon to act in a partisan manner, in the strict political sense, using power and social influence to change society. In the name of pastoral action the official church forms a temporal pressure group and the ministers assume socio-political leadership.

This Christology likewise does not correspond to the deeds and to the true nature of Jesus' messiahship. Things are not quite so simple and Christ's position toward the society of his time and toward the liberation of his people was much more profound than what appears at first sight. It is significant that Jesus has been linked to both the Zealots and the Essenes, and that today it can be shown, without a doubt, that he did not participate in either of these movements (see especially M. Hengel and others in *Evangelische Kommentare,* 1969: "The interpretation, again popular, of Jesus as a political-social revolutionary connected with the Zealots is based on a one-sided interpretation that does violence to the sources").

To situate authentically the mission of Christ in relation to the political situation of his time, we need to apply to this question the mystery of the Incarnation. To speak of a redemptive-historical Incarnation of the Son of God is not just to affirm that God became man at a determined and identifiable time and place. It is to affirm also that Jesus came to participate in some way in the historical, religious, social, and political movements of his time and that these movements influenced and conditioned his activity.

Specifically, if we do not want to fall into a sort of disguised Monophysitism, we must accept the fact that Jesus was a Jew, subject to the conflicts and aspirations prevalent in the Palestine of his day. Subject to the Romans like the rest of the Jews, he shared their desires for liberation, subject to the pressures of the social, political, and religious movements that we mentioned earlier. His attitudes and his preaching touched on the political question of his day, and he could hardly avoid coming into conflict with both the pharisaic religious powers and the civil authorities.[4] In this sense it becomes clear that his trial before the Sanhedrin and before Pilate took the historical form of a political trial. "We caught this man perverting our nation, and forbidding us to give tribute to Caesar, and saying that he himself is Christ, the King. . . . He stirs up the people."[5] "Anyone who makes himself a king sets himself against Caesar."[6] Even the way of his death had a political nuance. It is well known that the cross was a torture reserved especially for subversives.

Moreover, in the messiahship of Jesus there is no seeking for anything temporal or political, and he himself avoided being taken as a social leader. This is so clear in all Christological tradition that it is unnecessary to enlarge upon it. His message contains no program or strategy of political liberation. Jesus was fundamentally a religious leader who announced the kingdom of God as a religious, pastoral message. Not by his stance before the established authority,[7] or in the content of his preaching (the eschatological kingdom of God and the message of the beatitudes), or in the orientation he gave to his disciples did there appear anything comparable to a political messiah or a social leader.

But still he was thought of by many people, including

the disciples and apostles, as a political, temporal messiah
to the point that one of the chief preoccupations of Jesus
was to dispel this false impression.[8]

We should look for the answer not only in the Jews'
fervent expectation of a messiah who would be a political
liberator. Above all we should seek it in the very nature of
Christ's message. In announcing the kingdom of God and
the reconciliation of human beings with the Father
through the redemption of all sin, Jesus reveals the destiny
and the demands for conversion of people and societies.
The kingdom of God as a promise that even now is present
among us[9] implants in society values that will allow for the
criticism of all forms of social and structural sin, including
all forms of exploitation and domination. Thus, the
preaching of the kingdom is not properly speaking a political discourse, but it can give rise to authentic liberation
movements among human beings: insofar as it makes
them conscious of various sinful situations and insofar as
it inspires them to transform society because of a Gospel
of the kingdom in which they have believed.

In this sense, the religious-pastoral message of Jesus
gave rise to a dynamic of social changes for his time and
for all time to come. The socio-political order is a dimension of the very proclamation of the Christian faith, which
is contemplation, commitment, and a personal and social
criticism of all that would separate us from the kingdom.
In this very precise sense the action of Christ—and the
action of the church—is involved with the political order,
insofar as they are called upon to bring about changes in
the political systems.

Therefore, the religious messiahship of Jesus was sus-
ceptible to confusion. Developing in a society oppressed
in many ways, it could not but appear as critical of a
system both religiously and civilly totalitarian, thus un-
leashing hopes of a temporal liberator. This same Christ-

ological danger is also ecclesiological in that the church, whose pastoral activity has the same characteristics, can be attracted toward political power and a purely temporal liberation. This, evidently, is a constant temptation of pastoral activity.

THE TEMPTATION OF POWER
AND "POLITICAL ACTION"

This temptation is not proper only to the hierarchy of the church and its pastoral activity. Because of the close solidarity that exists between true religious messiahship and temporal messiahship, this was the fundamental temptation of the public life of Jesus. We have already spoken of the highly politicized situation of Israel and expectations of liberation from the Roman rule. We have spoken of how the people and Jesus' followers to the very end desired him to be a temporal savior of Israel and their king. In this sense the death of Christ was a collective frustration.

The temptation to be a political messiah assailed Jesus not only externally but internally as well. His messianic consciousness was constantly besieged, as is clearly shown in the triple temptation on the mountain after his forty days in the desert.[10] To change stones into bread simply to satisfy hunger; to cast himself down from the pinnacle of the temple to demonstrate his divine power; to gain possession of all the kingdoms of the world and their glory in exchange for the acceptance of Satan's power— these are all forms of one single temptation: that of renouncing the power of the Word and of evangelical means of action in order to give himself to ways of temporal and political pressure. This demon was constantly confronting the mission of Jesus[11] and caused a crisis in the agony in the garden the night of the Passion.[12] The temptation of Jesus in Gethsemane is of this same kind; the chalice that he had to accept was that of redeeming and freeing people through the poverty and the destruction of the cross and not through any spectacular success of a political messiahship.

It ought not to surprise us then that the temptation to power and to political action is prevalent also among the ministers of the church in their pastoral activity. They are activities that dovetail in many aspects and there is no greater temptation than that of substitution. (Just as angelism and the lack of temporal commitment is the temptation of the contemplative, Machiavellism is that of the Christian revolutionary).

The ever-present risk of politicizing the evangelical mission of the church and the abuses that are always— even today—made of this mission ought not to cause a contrary reaction. Just as Christ did not avoid the painful consequences and the conflicts with the system brought about by the proclamation of the Gospel, pastoral activity should never lose its socio-political challenge, which is part of its very essence. The apostolate, bearer of an eschatological-incarnational message, follows the laws of Christology. In Christology, in the sense that we have explained, it finds its true liberating significance, in the path of Christ, who liberates completely, including from temporal oppression—although through non-political mediations. And so Jesus remains truly the way and the model of all Christian commitment to liberation, the prophetic figure in the liberation of his people and of *the little ones* throughout history. "The Spirit has sent me to bring the Good News to the poor, . . . to set at liberty those who are oppressed. . . ."[13]

THE MESSAGE OF JESUS AS LIBERATOR OF ISRAEL

The liberating temporal consequences of Jesus' message in the society of his time were due to the fact that it sowed in the Roman system the lasting seeds of liberty and community.

To proclaim the one, true God as Father of all puts an end to any idolatry. It relativizes people and values that in that society took the absolute place of God: in the first place, the emperor and his authority, cornerstone of the cohesion and of the mythical power of the empire. It destroys the ideological bases of its totalitarianism. Along with this, it gives each person a sense of dignity and equality before the political authority, firmly establishing the ultimate bases of participation and solidarity. Even beyond this, Jesus does away with the concept of theocracy and of a theocratic state—whether Christian or secular—the foundation of absolute and oppressive systems. "Render to Caesar the things that are Caesar's and to God the things that are God's. . . ."[14] With this phrase Jesus desacralizes political power, striking out at the same time against Jewish theocracy and against Roman totalitarianism.

These are struck down at their very foundations, not through a maneuver of political strategy, but through the proclamation of the truth about God and humanity, a truth that is prophetic, that unmasks injustices, that makes us free.[15] Socially and politically, this undercuts evil, both in the short and the long term. More than the ambitions of the Zealots, and more than any revolutionary plan or action, Jesus destroys the very bases of the imperial system.

In the second place, the message of Jesus is a liberating one because he summoned the poor to form his kingdom in a privileged way. He even proclaimed that one had to become poor in spirit in order to enter the kingdom.[16]

In the cultural context of his time, this could not help but have deep socio-political repercussions. Practically speaking, it set into motion and gave a certain mystique and social power to a group hitherto neglected and without social significance. It introduced into the empire and into the aristocratic society that this group had given rise to a new power, conscious of its own dignity, independent of the system and of the established authorities, and desirous of establishing justice. This new force would be decisive in the weakening and collapse of the empire. This call to the *little ones* to establish the kingdom will be at the root of all authentic liberation movements.

In the third place, Jesus proclaims his kingdom as universal, fulfilling the prophecies. He breaks through the limits of Jewish nationalism and of a salvation exclusively for them.[17] He thus overcomes the tribalism of the Pharisees and the Zealots, sending forth his disciples on a universal mission that carries them to the heart of the empire as well as beyond its borders. This dynamism not only eroded the traditional Jewish religious, nationalistic, and sectarian system. It also made its influence felt in all strata of the imperial society and of all future totalitarian societies.

In short, in proclaiming the condition of the new human being in the Sermon on the Mount and in the beatitudes, Jesus created a new prophetic consciousness in his disciples. He renewed their vocation to equality and community, demanding of them values that were diametrically opposed to those promoted by the dominant social system. To the extent that the values proposed by the beatitudes penetrate the hearts of people and of society, they will condemn any socio-political structure incompatible with those ideals.

Without putting forth a model for a better society, or a concrete program of liberation, Jesus creates a movement of liberation and fraternity that we find at the origin of many later social changes.

It is for this reason that the religious messiahship of Jesus and his predominantly eschatological mission could

not avoid being accused of *being involved in politics* and of
his being a *worldly messiahship*. This temptation of ambiguity remains even today, having been transferred to the
mission of the church. Without being a politician and
without wishing to assume any temporal leadership, Jesus
is an authentic liberator in the deepest sense of the word,
even including the social consequences. And he is a
dangerous liberator, more dangerous for the oppressing
powers—political and religious—than the revolutionary politicians, the Zealots, and others. Whatever might
be the exegetical judgment regarding the historical fact,
the confrontation of Jesus with Barabbas the day of
the crucifixion is very significant in this respect.[18] The
message the Gospel gives us, from the point of view of our
present discussion, is sufficiently clear. Barabbas was an
important prisoner. Given the antecedents and the political context of Israel, today many agree that he was a
revolutionary, a subversive, a Zealot. They had to choose
between the freeing of Jesus or a political revolutionary.
And the leaders preferred to set Barabbas free. For the
system Jesus is more dangerous than a revolutionary and
his message is more subversive than a political proclamation.

A reading of the life of Christ that takes into account the
political context in which it developed makes it evident,
then, that it is the inspiration and model for all those
Christians committed to liberation through prophetic,
rather than political, means. The socio-political dimension of Christology is undeniable, as are the temporal
consequences of the kingdom that Christ announced. It is
very important today to take into account this dimension
of Jesus in a theology as well as in a spirituality of liberation. It is equally obvious that this socio-political dimension of Christology does not exhaust either the mission or
the message of Jesus. The Lord also announced personal

conversion, the forgiveness of sins, reconciliation with the Father, the cross, the kingdom, the future life, etc. What we mean is that if we do not deepen our understanding of the *political* dimensions of the messiahship of Jesus, many Christians, in their temporal commitments, will find themselves in great difficulties with their faith, believers in a Christ who has no meaning for the liberation in history of the *little ones*.

XI

Mary, Follower of Jesus

The Almighty has done great things for me.
Holy is his name,
and his mercy reaches from age to age for those who
* fear him.*
He has shown the power of his arm,
he has routed the proud of heart.
He has pulled down princes from their thrones and
* exalted the lowly.*
The hungry he has filled with good things, the rich
* sent empty away.*[1]

Paradoxically, there is in Latin America a pastoral crisis in regard to the most deeply rooted devotions. The traditional devotion to the cross meets with a difficulty at times insurmountable to find a "preaching of the cross" that is liberating. Devotion to Mary, which has never lost its meaning and its popular appeal, is also coming up against a pastoral approach confused and incapable of adequately responding to the religious spirit of our peoples.

The cause of the Marian crisis is complex: sociological, anthropological, theological, spiritual, pastoral. It must be remembered that the transformation of our society brought with it a change in cultural expressions and sentiments. The religious figure of the Virgin Mary was solidly

110

entrenched in our traditional rural culture, and the ways in which this devotion was expressed no longer satisfy the Latin American youth.

"Feminine anthropology" has been radically transformed in the last twenty-five years. The social and psychological significance of the contemporary woman made the preaching and symbols of the Virgin Mary violently anachronistic. Suddenly it seems that pastoral programs do not now know how to place her, how to present her as a model to new generations and how to generate affection for the Mother of Jesus.

There are reasons for this based in our spiritual theology. Personally, I think that the "Monophysite" tendency that, according to many, contaminated Iberian Catholicism has also left its stamp on devotion to Mary. If Christ's divinity was so accentuated that "Jesus the man" and the incarnate and human aspects of the Lord were left in shadows, the same seems to have happened with the Mother of God. Her prerogatives, her privileges, her power, and dogmatic truths were accentuated. This "maximization" presented Mary in the evangelization of the Latin American people as a "demigod." It often replaced the mediation of Christ and made foreign to preaching the whole human dimension of a woman of our race, saved from sin and led by God through faith, suffering, and poverty. The privileges minimized her service and her human significance.

The Church of Vatican II did away with this extremism in order to create a correct balance. This left preachers and catechists now confused by socio-cultural and psychological changes, practically without arms.

Some began to create false dilemmas: Should we speak of Christ or of Mary? To which of the two ought we to teach the people to pray? Obviously these are rationalizations of an "enlightened" Christianity, since in the

Catholic community structure the same thing occurs as in
a family where the children do not reason out whether
they should speak to the father or the mother. In this
context, the ecumenical movement added to the crisis,
inhibiting a Marian pastoral activity on all fronts.

The crisis over devotion to Mary is not a crisis of our
popular Catholicism but rather a pastoral crisis. Mary is
part of our profane history, both popular and heroic. She
is part of our culture, both Spanish and indigenous. She
deeply influences our Catholicism from Mexico to Chile.
More than a doctrine taught by the church, Mary has been
the great adopted one of the Latin American people. Our
present pastoral task is to reinterpret this adoption in such
a way that it may be as significant for the new generations
as it was for the previous ones. It is to rescue the liberating
significance (of which Christians were so conscious—
according to the mentality of their time—during the first
evangelization and the independence movement)   that
today is often imprisoned by the interests of politicians
and reactionaries and by narrow nationalism.

THE FAITHFUL MOTHER

"If we do not return to the Gospel, Jesus does not live in
us," a saintly contemporary has said. It should also be
said that if we do not return to the Gospel, we will not
rediscover Mary. There we find the secret of her blessedness and of her significance for the church and for future
generations. The Gospel shows us, in the seriousness of
its stories, her radical faith, her unyielding confidence that
extends beyond disconcerting appearances, her commitment to a call that led her to loneliness and to the cross, an
altogether authentic follower of Jesus.

This faithful follower of Jesus is also his mother and his
most intimate collaborator. For this reason she gives to

Christianity, once and for all, not only the grace of the greatest fidelity but the charismatic grace of the fidelity of a woman-mother. In the church the maternity of Mary is not a theological doctrine superimposed on the human and religious aspirations of certain peoples. We are so accustomed to it that, as with the air we breathe, we can forget its profound significance in our existence.

In the organism of the life of faith, this feminine-maternal charisma is essential. If it were lacking, Christianity, as God wanted it to be historically, would be terribly deformed. The very experience of fidelity to Jesus' word, which constitutes the essence of our religion, would lose decisive dimensions. The Gospel itself, which makes this experience known to us, would be deprived of its best living commentary, the complete fidelity of a woman to Jesus Christ.

In order that Christianity be rich and complete, it must reflect the values of this fidelity, the capacity of a complete giving of oneself, of absolute abandonment to the love and promises of God. Mary's fidelity, fruit of this confidence and total giving of self to the Word of God, gives to Christianity the maternal-feminine dimension of the following of Christ, making it an integral part of the experience of faith.

There is, therefore, a profound anthropological reason for the association of Mary with the work of Christ: on the level of Christian existence also it is true that "together with the work of a great man will be found a great woman."

As a type of the Christian woman, she has in the church as well the pedagogical role that goes along with this symbol. The church, of which she is mother and model, is called upon by her presence to become human and familiar, since it is proper for the woman to be a current of affection. If our popular church in Latin America is more communitarian than juridical and institutional, more affective and intuitive than rationalistic, this is due in great part to Mary. Because the maternity of Mary is not an abstract dogma among the people; it has the pedagogical role of bringing steadfastness and confidence, of loosing forces of creativity and humanity of a popular culture that has been habitually alienated.

POOR AND ONE WITH THE PEOPLE

This people has been able to identify itself with the Mother of God. It has also seen in her a woman of the people, poor and united with its aspirations. It has been able to go beyond the sociological poverty of Mary to see in her the sign of her radical interior poverty. On delving into the message of the poor Virgin, a sign and condition of the freedom of the heart, those that look for their liberation and development will be able to avoid the ambiguities of materialism and of alienation, taking upon themselves the demands of an interior liberation.

The church's teaching on liberation tells us that for Latin America Mary signifies a new human being. Mary, identified with her people is, in her fidelity, her poverty, and her commitment, the sign and the hope that this is possible. In this woman of Nazareth, the poor see one of their race overcome the confusion, the anguish, and the sense of failure, temptations that assailed Mary from the moment of her acceptance of her commitment at the annunciation until its completion on Calvary. Because there was always latent in her the "eschatological clause" of Christian commitment, she can incarnate for all suffering generations the hope in the triumph of justice and peace, the triumph of reconciliation over division, of the new person over enslavements.

The religiosity of Mary is not in the least alienating, for in the hope of her commitment she is aware that justice and reconciliation imply the vindication of the poor and oppressed. In the Magnificat, in continuity with Isaiah and the prophets and anticipating the beatitudes, she hopes for a God who will put down the rich and the mighty and will exalt the poor and the lowly; Mary thus takes on the historic and conflictive conditions of her commitment. The hope of Mary is not personal and eschatological; it refers equally to a change of the structures that impede the historic realization of the promises of God.

To use an expression often heard in Latin American Christianity today, Mary appears as one committed to the liberation of all people, particularly the most oppressed. For this reason she experienced poverty, suffering, flight, and exile. The Gospel accounts of her humiliation in Bethlehem, her persecution by Herod, her exile in Egypt, and her sufferings on Calvary are not pious biblical stories. They are the signs of her faithfulness to the commitment she accepted at the time of the Annunciation. In this, also, Mary is typical of the church, insofar as the church will remain faithful to the integrity of its mission. She is also typical of the Christian communities as "exodus" and as an "Abrahamic minority," and in them she maintains the hope and the strength to await the hour of the liberating God.

It is in this spirit that Mary accompanied the early communities and today continues to accompany all Christian communities that struggle with hope for the coming of the kingdom of God. She accompanies them as a faithful witness of the new person and of the new church that they are building, since it is the task of witnesses to show with the testimony of their lives what others still hope for. She accompanies them as a pilgrim, since she also walked the route of the exodus that they now walk, and like them she grew in faith, hope, and love. For it is proper for pilgrims to forge ahead toward the reality they hope for.

On this road, like every creature who lives by faith, the

word of Jesus was her guide and her comfort. Mary, the contemplative pilgrim, lived thus in a constant "review of life," keeping in her heart the words and deeds that she shared with her Son.

For Mary, the gift of her maternity and of her constant association with the work of Christ was not given to her only as a privilege or a miracle. It was for her a commitment and a service to Jesus and to all humanity. She receives it with a humble heart as a gift of participation in the mission of Jesus. Mary in her attitude enhances the category of "gift" that Christianity has, a gift that always leads to commitment.

The faithful Virgin adhered absolutely to the mission with which the Father associated her, with the risk and the option of faith that always comes with the acceptance of the word of God spoken to us. Her privileges and her historic mission form part of the same commitment, and she is blessed rather for her faithfulness in welcoming and devoting herself to the mission that God offered her.[2]

THE VIRGIN OF RECONCILIATION

The Gospel figure of Mary is rich in values that can nourish in a new way the devotion and the commitment of new generations of Christians. In the case of popular religiosity, this possibility is reinforced, as we have noted, by the unity of values and attitudes that exists between Mary and the people. With her the poor are at home and in her they can see religion in the concrete, in daily life, close to the poor.

It is in this context that we must evaluate the popular devotion to Mary in all its pastoral meaning, which has its greatest sign in the Marian shrines throughout the continent. They are the meeting places for Mary and the people, where their unity becomes an event. In them Mary shows herself together with the poor; she emerges from the place where they live.

Mary's choice of "the place of the poor" as her dwelling place is brought out in popular Catholicism by the accounts of the apparitions of the Virgin, which frequently give rise to these sanctuaries. Whether this or that account is legendary or has a historical foundation is of secondary importance for Marian pastoral activity. What is important is to redeem what the people want to express and what they can learn from those accounts: Mary reveals herself to the poor, in poor places, she remains forever among them, and she uses the poor to evangelize the rich and powerful. The "apparition" and the shrine among the poor calls the rich into question at the same time that it gives security to the oppressed. It gives status to the humble and disposes the powerful to hear. The tradition of the Magnificat is repeated in popular religiosity: "He has put down the mighty from their thrones and has raised up the lowly; he has filled the hungry with good things and the rich he has sent away empty."[3]

Popular pastoral planning in Latin America is confronted today with the challenge of evangelizing multitudes of neglected peoples, neglected by pastoral institutions but not at all orphans. The multitudes are not neglected by Mary, who constitutes a great pastoral hope and a guide for evangelization.

The very way in which Mary is situated among the poor and the neglected—on the social and ecclesial periphery —serves us as a model and a criterion for evangelization. It teaches us that the starting point of any popular pastoral program is the placement of the evangelizers in the midst of the poor, establishing among them their "sanctuary." Like Mary, evangelizers need to be "adopted" by the people, in a mutual listening, acceptance, and identification. The adoption is more than just an adaptation; it presupposes the acceptance and recognition of the evangelizer by the people as "one of them."

From this perspective, evangelization doesn't come from "the center" (the rich and powerful) to adapt to the "periphery"; it comes, rather, from the "periphery," which has a message to give to "the center." Since the neglected have no means to make themselves heard and taken seriously, their message is Mary. The light of the message of the poor, faithful, and committed Virgin, Mother of us all, is the language of evangelization "for" and "from" the poor. The understanding of this message by the rich is the source of their liberation. It enables them to discover the world of the poor and become sensitive to the need for justice and reconciliation. It challenges their right to make themselves a "dominant center."

The symbol of this reconciliation can be found in the pilgrimages of rich and poor to the places of devotion to Mary, which are found among the neglected. The movement towards Mary goes thus from "the center" to "the periphery." It obliges the rich to go out of themselves and to meet the poor. It gives to the poor a sense of security and obliges them to meet the rich with no complexes, on an equal footing. Mary is, then, like a type of the popular church and of popular pastoral activity, one of the rare symbols of integration in Latin American society. I say symbol, because for the evangelization of the rich through service and "pilgrimage" toward the poor, a purely material journey is not enough. Every journey toward the place of Mary among the neglected is a symbol of a change of attitude, of an interior journey. It means to make oneself poor with Mary and then to accept, like her, participation in Jesus' work of liberation.

In the Latin American society of today, apparently so far from its socio-political liberation, Mary is a symbol of a form of religious liberation, popular and possible in any political contingency: liberation by way of integration into a cultural and religious family and by way of reconciliation with our own values, identified in Mary.

Popular liberation, integrally Christian, is the exodus from any type of enslavement. Radical slavery, the sin of alienation that is at the basis of the oppression of a people, is that of manipulating them, "exiling" a people from itself, from its roots, from its values, from its history. Sin is disintegration, and liberation is reconciliation with God, with brother and sister, with society, basically with one's own self. It is a process of reintegration toward a new person and a new society, a process that coincides with fidelity to the values of the kingdom of God and with the religious mission of the church.

In the church, as we have already said, Mary's charism as mother-teacher, who identifies herself with her neglected and insecure people, is decisive. The great error of "elitist" and sophisticated pastoral programs is to have divorced the aspirations of the people from the ecclesial role of Mary. This role has been reduced to general, dogmatic truths without psychological or social repercussions in the soul of the people, or to peripheral devotions, based on the subjectivity of religious sentiment, and thus ambiguous when confronted with the evangelization and growth of faith of a committed people. The only possible way to correct this kind of Marian "Monophysitism" is to rediscover her in the Gospel, in the best Catholic tradition, as the incarnation of the new person and of the new church. Through her faith in Jesus, she gives birth to an integrally liberating and educating commitment that comes from the heart of the masses. Because of this Mary understands poverty, risk, solidarity with the weak, exile, and the cross, in the certain hope of the triumph of Christ the liberator.

Notes

CHAPTER I

1. John 21.
2. Matt. 8:18-22; 9:9; 10:38; 12:24; 19:21, 28; Mark 1:17, 18; 3:13, 14; Luke 14:25-27; John 1:43; 8:12; 10:1-6, 27; 21:15-22, etc.
3. John 21.
4. Matt. 13:44-46.
5. Matt. 7:22-25.
6. Luke 5:1-11.
7. John 1:35-42.
8. Luke 5:11.
9. Matt. 16:16.
10. Matt. 20:21; Mark 9:34.
11. Acts 1:6.
12. Matt. 16:22.
13. Mark 9:14-29.
14. Matt. 26:33-35.
15. John 21:1-19.
16. John 21:15-17.
17. John 21:18.
18. Luke 18:27.
19. Acts 1:8.
20. John 12:25.
21. John 21:18.

CHAPTER II

1. John 1:14-16.
2. 1 Cor. 1:30; Eph. 1:9.
3. Phil. 3:8.
4. Gal. 1:16.
5. 1 John 1:1.
6. Mark 1:35; Luke 4:42, etc.
7. Matt. 9:20ff.
8. John 6:15.
9. John 13:1.
10. Luke 4:40.
11. Mark 10:14.
12. John 4:1ff.
13. Matt. 26:50.
14. John 2:26.
15. Matt. 7:29.
16. John 11:48.
17. Phil. 2:6ff.
18. John 6:66ff.
19. John 10:18.
20. Matt. 25:40.
21. 1 Cor. 1:25.
22. John 14:9.

CHAPTER III

1. Luke 10:27-29.
2. John 13:34; Matt. 23:8-9.
3. Luke 10:27; John 15:12.
4. Luke 10:25ff.
5. Luke 10:29.
6. Luke 10:37.
7. Luke 10:30-35.
8. Matt. 25:31ff.
9. Matt. 25:40.
10. Luke 10:36.
11. Luke 10:37.
12. Luke 10:31.
13. Luke 10:3-35.
14. John 4:9.
15. Luke 10:37.

CHAPTER IV

1. Matt. 25:37-40.
2. Matt. 25.

120

3. Matt. 25:34ff.
4. Isaiah 1:10-17; 58:6-7, etc.
5. Luke 4:18-19.
6. Luke 7:22.
7. Luke 14:33.
8. Matt. 6:24.
9. Matt. 6:24.
10. Matt. 6:19-21.
11. Luke 18:24.
12. Luke 6:24-25.
13. Apoc. 3:17.
14. Luke 18:27.
15. Luke 19:10.
16. Luke 12:21.
17. Matt. 6:11.
18. Luke 12:18.
19. James 5:1ff.
20. Matt. 6:25-33.
21. Matt. 24:45.
22. Luke 19:8.
23. Offertory prayer.
24. John 3:17.
25. Luke 19:8.
26. Luke 10:35.
27. Luke 16:1-9.
28. Luke 16:9.
29. Mark 14:3ff.
30. Matt. 6:25ff.

CHAPTER V

1. John 4:10, 14.
2. Ibid.
3. John 3:5ff.
4. Hebrews.

CHAPTER VI

1. Matt. 25:37–40.
2. John 1:1.
3. Matt. 17:1ff.
4. 2 Cor. 12; Phil. 3:7ff., etc.
5. Matt. 25:31.
6. Rom. 6:1.
7. St. John of the Cross.
8. Matt. 4:1.
9. Gal. 1:17.
10. Ezek. 1ff.; 1 Kings; Elijah, etc.
11. Num. 14, 20.
12. Heb. 11:26-27.
13. Matt. 25:41.

CHAPTER VII

1. Matt. 26:36-39.
2. John 10:18.
3. John 1:14.
4. Luke 14:27.
5. St. John.
6. Luke 4:18.
7. Mark 3:10.
8. Mark 6:30.
9. Luke 4:42.; John 6:15, etc.
10. Matt. 5:1.
11. Luke 5:3.
12. Matt. 14:21.
13. John 2:25.
14. John 6:15.
15. Luke 4:13.
16. John 6:15.
17. John 6:26ff.
18. John 6:41.
19. John 6:52.
20. John 6:66-70.
21. John 7:1.
22. Mark 10:33.
23. John 11:16.
24. Mark 10:32.
25. Matt. 21:8ff.
26. Mark 12:12.
27. Luke 22:39-46.

CHAPTER VIII

1. Luke 9:61.
2. Rev. 2:3.
3. Rev. 3:15ff.
4. Mark 3:21.
5. Matt. 5:13.
6. Matt. 5:17-20.
7. Matt. 10:37-39.
8. Matt. 18:8.
9. Matt. 13:44-46.
10. Matt. 6:24; Luke 12:21, 34.
11. Matt. 7:13.
12. Luke 9:57-62.
13. Matt. 26:25-26.
14. Matt. 11:12.
15. Matt. 16:21-24; 17:15.
16. John 3:3.
17. Matt. 18:4.
18. Matt. 20:26.
19. John 12:24-26.

20. Matt. 10:22-25; 18:21; John 15:19-25; 16:1.
21. Matt. 10:34-35.
22. Luke 2:34; John 7:12-13.
23. Luke 11:23.
24. John 9:39.
25. Matt. 11:6.
26. Luke 6:20-26.
27. Luke 6:23.
28. Matt. 5:22.
29. Matt. 7:1.
30. Matt. 5:37-48; 6:14.
31. John 13:34; Mark 12:33; John 15:13.
32. Luke 14:12; 17:10.
33. Luke 10:25ff.
34. Matt. 25:40.
35. Matt. 11:25.
36. Matt. 14:25ff.
37. Matt. 17:20; 21:21.
38. Matt. 7:7-11; Mark 9:23-29; Luke 11:5ff.; John 15:16
39. Luke 14:33.
40. Matt. 6:25-34.
41. Matt. 19:23.
42. Matt. 10:10.
43. Luke 2:7-8.
44. Mark 6:2-3; John 1:46; 7:15.
45. Matt. 5:37.
46. Matt. 26:64; 27:11; Luke 22:67ff.; John 18:37ff.
47. Mark 7:3-13.
48. Matt. 23:1ff.; Mark 2:27; Matt. 9:14; 11:16; 12:1ff.; 15:7-11; 17:24.
49. Matt. 19:30; 20:12-15.
50. Matt. 21:31.
51. Luke 7:36ff.
52. Mark 12:41-44.
53. Luke 18:9.
54. Luke 10:38.

55. John 10:15-18; 13:1.
56. Luke 2:49.
57. John 13:1.
58. Matt. 3:14; John 13:4ff.
59. Matt. 26:51; 27:12; 27:40-44; 4:1ff.; Mark 14:61; 15:5; John 18:22.

CHAPTER IX

1. John 8:31-32.

CHAPTER X

1. Luke 4:18–19.
2. Luke 9:54.
3. John 11:48.
4. John 11:47ff.
5. Luke 23:2, 5.
6. John 19:12.
7. John 18:33-37; Luke 20:20-25, etc.
8. Matt. 16:22ff.; John 6:15; Matt. 20:22ff.; Acts 1:6, etc.
9. Mark 1:14-15.
10. Matt. 4:1-11.
11. Matt. 16:23; John 6:15.
12. Matt. 26:39ff.
13. Luke 4:18.
14. Matt. 22:21.
15. John 8:32.
16. Matt. 5:3; Luke 6:20; 16:19ff.; 18:18ff., etc.
17. Matt. 24:14; 21:43ff.
18. Matt. 27:15ff.

CHAPTER XI

1. Luke 1:49–53.
2. Luke 11:28.
3. Luke 1:52.